Vernacular Bibles in Africa through European Eyes

In reflecting with insight on the convergence of ontological, epistemological and socio-historical forces in two sub-Saharan African Bible translations of the missionary era, Dr. Nyirenda highlights challenges inherent to the integrity of the translation process when superiority is assumed and when constructs that were relevant in their own context, such as the Enlightenment and the evangelistic impetus of the Great Awakening, are uncritically transferred to another context and to other agendas. In so doing he makes a valuable cautionary contribution to the Bible translation conversation also in the current post-missionary paradigm.

Dirk Gevers
Secretary General,
United Bible Societies

This is a first rate and impressive piece of original research and writing by an expert in the field. The Rev. Dr. Misheck Nyirenda has worked for many years as a biblical and linguistic consultant in the field of Bible translation and has overseen many translations in African languages under the auspices of the United Bible Societies. From his base in Zambia, Dr. Nyirenda has wide and deep first-hand knowledge and understanding of Bible translation work in Africa. He is clearly well positioned to view the history of Bible translation in Africa from a privileged position, both as an African and as an expert in the field. This book is authoritative, insightful, informative and timely. Books such as this one, by African scholars, are indeed rare. This is undoubtedly a most welcome text. It will help to fill the gap as well as meet the need for information and update this important subject. Readers of this book will no doubt be indebted to Dr. Nyirenda for taking on this urgent and most needed task. I found this work inspiring, insightful, handy and invaluable.

Aloo Osotsi Mojola, PhD
Professor of Philosophy and Translation Studies,
St Paul's University, Kenya
Formerly Translation Consultant and Africa Translation Coordinator,
United Bible Societies

Misheck Nyirenda has put together a most fascinating book: history, perspective, ideology and contemporary scholarship – all blended together. I have reread several chapters out of pleasure due to the way his frank and incisive approach has made a book on the history, theory, practice and politics of Bible translation come alive. The reader rapidly gains a broad understanding and appreciation of factors which have shaped this kind of work, especially in Africa. *Vernacular Bibles in Africa through European Eyes* inspires a rethink of Bible translation in terms of hegemony, agency, the place of orality and what he calls "polarity versus holism." Indeed, it is impossible not to draw parallels between the now and the then of Bible translation especially with respect to having the target populations critically participate at the level of text and exegesis.

Margaret Jepkirui Muthwii, PhD
Vice Chancellor and Professor of Languages and Linguistics,
Pan Africa Christian University, Kenya

In this innovative and very important volume on the history of two Bible translations in Africa – one in West Africa and one in East Africa – Misheck Nyirenda examines the epistemology at play in the Bible translation process and thereby provides much-needed knowledge for a lacune in the history of translation studies and the theory of Bible translation. Invaluable lessons can be learned which will have huge impact on future Bible translations.

In light of the nineteenth-century missionary translators who shared the same European epistemological viewpoint and methodology, especially with respect to their approach to developing orthographies for conveying the written word of God in African languages, Nyirenda cautions that twenty-first-century Bible translation efforts in Africa may similarly be subject to hegemonic European epistemologies. This error will be repeated if African Bible translators are not fully capable of reading the biblical source texts in their original languages considering their cultural contexts, if analysis of African target languages is not conducted by those who know those languages, and if African translators are not aware of their own epistemologies of knowledge. The volume is an indispensable read for scholars in translation studies and Bible translators.

Cynthia L. Miller-Naudé, PhD, and Jacobus A. Naudé, PhD
Senior Professors of Hebrew,
University of the Free State, South Africa

Vernacular Bibles in Africa through European Eyes

Case Studies in Nineteenth-Century Translation

Misheck Nyirenda

© 2023 Misheck Nyirenda

Published 2023 by HippoBooks, an imprint of ACTS and Langham Publishing.

Africa Christian Textbooks (ACTS), TCNN, PMB 2020, Bukuru 930008, Plateau State, Nigeria
www.actsnigeria.org
Langham Publishing, PO Box 296, Carlisle, Cumbria CA3 9WZ, UK
www.langham.org

ISBNs:
978-1-83973-252-2 Print
978-1-83973-915-6 ePub
978-1-83973-916-3 PDF

Misheck Nyirenda has asserted his right under the Copyright, Designs and Patents Act, 1988 to be identified as the Author of this work.

All rights reserved. No part of this publication may be reproduced, stored in a retrieval system or transmitted, in any form or by any means, electronic, mechanical, photocopying, recording or otherwise, without the prior written permission of the publisher or the Copyright Licensing Agency.

Requests to reuse content from Langham Publishing are processed through PLSclear. Please visit www.plsclear.com to complete your request.

Scripture marked (NASB) taken from the New American Standard Bible®, Copyright © 1960, 1962, 1963, 1968, 1971, 1972, 1973, 1975, 1977, 1995 by The Lockman Foundation. Used by permission.

All Scripture quotations marked (NET) are from the New English Translation (NET). NET Bible® copyright ©1996–2006 by Biblical Studies Press, L.L.C. www.bible.org. Used by permission. All rights reserved worldwide.

All Scripture quotations marked (NIV) are taken from the Holy Bible, New International Version®, Anglicised, NIV®. Copyright © 1979, 1984, 2011 by Biblica, Inc®. Used by permission. All rights reserved worldwide.

Scripture quotations marked (NLT) are taken from the Holy Bible, New Living Translation, copyright © 1996, 2004, 2007, 2013, 2015 by Tyndale House Foundation. Used by permission of Tyndale House Publishers, Inc., Carol Stream, Illinois 60188. All rights reserved.

Scripture quotations marked (RSV) are taken from the Revised Standard Version of the Bible, copyright © 1946, 1952, and 1971 National Council of the Churches of Christ in the United States of America. Used by permission. All rights reserved.

British Library Cataloguing-in-Publication Data
A catalogue record for this book is available from the British Library

ISBN: 978-1-83973-252-2

Cover & Book Design: projectluz.com

The publishers of this book actively support theological dialogue and an author's right to publish but do not necessarily endorse the views and opinions set forth here or in works referenced within this publication, nor guarantee technical and grammatical correctness. The publishers do not accept any responsibility or liability to persons or property as a consequence of the reading, use or interpretation of its published content.

I dedicate this book to the memory of three people who shared in the intellectual, social and spiritual realities embodied in this book. To the late Professor David A. Kerr, for pulling off the incredible feat of being a Scottish gentleman, noteworthy academic and extremely pleasant company. Non-Western scholarship was more than just an academic experiment to him. To Dr. Jack Thompson for embodying the spirit and heart of the Xhosa missionaries to Central Africa and to Dr. Andrew C. Ross for carrying Malawi and Africa in his heart to the end, and still managing to be an all-weather fan of Hibs United. A true *m'bale wanga*. Dr. Thompson and Dr. Ross have passed on, but their passion, fondness for Africa and their legacies there live on in my heart and in this book.

Contents

List of Abbreviations 1

Introduction 3

Part I: Background to Translation in the Nineteenth Century

1 An Overview of Bible Translation Theories from the Nineteenth Century to the Present 7

2 The Enlightenment, Mission and Imperialism 15

Part II: The Efik New Testament Bible Translation

3 The Historical Forces behind the Old Calabar Mission 31

4 Origins and History: Old Calabar Mission 45

5 Language and Translation Work 59

6 Translation and Translators 71

7 The Immediate Impact of the Translation on the Calabarese 77

Part III: The ChiChewa Bible Translation Project

8 Background to the Livingstonia and Blantyre Missions 85

9 Origins and History: Livingstonia and Blantyre Missions 93

10 Language and Translation Work 111

11 Evaluative Commentary on Laws' Translation of Mark 1:1–8 121

12 Laws' Translation of Mark 1:1–8 in the Light of Scott's and the Union Nyanja Translations 137

Part IV: Going Forward

13 Consequences of Developments Since the Twentieth Century 151

Appendix I: The New American Standard and Greek New Testament texts of Mark 1:1–8 163

Appendix II: Sample text of Laws' working translation of the Gospel of Mark, 1885 165

Appendix III: A copy of the letter of Robert Laws to the Rev. D. Knight, NBSS, 1928 167

Bibliography.. 169

List of Figures

Figure 1. Map of Old Calabar. 43

Figure 2. The Rev. Hugh Goldie and Rev. S. H. Edgerly, Old Calabar Mission. 65

Figure 3. Map of modern Malawi showing Blantyre and the successive headquarters of Livingstonia Mission: Cape Maclear, Bandawe and Livingstonia 92

Figure 4. The Rev. Dr. Robert Laws, Livingstonia Mission 117

Figure 5. The Union Nyanja Revision Panel. 1925 135

List of Abbreviations

BAGD	Bauer, Walter, William F. Arndt, F. Wilbur Gingrich, and Frederick W. Danker. *Greek English Lexicon of the New Testament and Other Early Christian Literature*, 2nd ed. Chicago: University of Chicago Press, 1979 (Bauer-Arndt-Gingirch-Danker)
BDB	Brown, Francis, S. R. Driver, and Charles A. Briggs. *A Hebrew and English Lexicon of the Old Testament* בח ספרי הברית החדשה. Jerusalem: The Bible Society in Israel, 2016
BHS	*Biblia Hebraica Stuttgartensia*. Edited by Karl Ellinger and Wilhelm Rudolph. Stuttgart: Deutsche Bibelgesellschaft, 1967–77
ESV	Holy Bible, English Standard Version
GNT	*The Greek New Testament*, Third edition (Corrected). Edited by Kurt Aland et al. Stuttgart: United Bible Societies, 1983
KJV	Holy Bible, King James Version, 1769 Blayney Edition of the 1611 King James Version of the Bible
LXX	*Septuaginta*. Edited by Alfred Ralphs. Stuttgart: Deutsche Bibelgesellschaft, 1979.
NAS	Holy Bible. New American Standard. The Lockman Foundation, 1977
NBSS	National Bible Society of Scotland
NET	Holy Bible, Net Bible
NIV	Holy Bible, New International Version
NLT	Holy Bible, New Living Translation
RGS	Royal Geographic Society
RSV	Holy Bible, Revised Standard Version
UP	United Presbyterian (Church)

Introduction

The substance of this book is multidisciplinary and can be discussed from the point of view of various academic interests including philosophy, colonial history, Christian mission, politics, biblical studies and Bible translation. It is necessary, therefore, to define and locate the discussion below, so that the appropriate lenses are applied in engaging it. The main interest here is Bible translation. This being the case, particular matters of interest will be touched upon as follows.

Foremost will be the philosophical constructs that formed the framework of the activities in this book. Coming to terms with these will require, to some degree, engagement with historical, political and social developments in the geographical areas of interest to this material: namely, Europe and Africa. This will naturally lead to discussion of the nature of the translation theories that the key personnel in the two projects under consideration held. However, in order to understand these theories in the context of other theories up to the present, it is necessary to provide a brief overview of Bible translation theories. In Part I we do this in the first chapter. This overview will be for comparative purposes only, with what was current during the nineteenth century.

In chapter 2 we narrow the background discussion to the state of epistemology in nineteenth-century Europe, the sending context of the missionaries who became the primary agents of Bible translation in nineteenth-century Africa. This discussion will provide the immediate framework for evaluating the activities of the two main characters in this book, Hugh Goldie and Robert Laws, in Parts II and III.

Greek επιστημη, "understanding" or "knowledge,"[1] is the etymological root of the subject of this book, a consideration of the role of epistemology in Bible translation in specific times and contexts. Specifically, this book seeks to demonstrate that Hugh Goldie and Robert Laws, the Scottish Presbyterian missionaries who translated the Efik New Testament of 1862 in Old Calabar and the Nyanja translation of Mark in 1885 in Central Africa respectively, assumed a common epistemology for all languages in their translation method.

---

1. BAGD, 300.

To demonstrate this, the book will consider two fundamental constituents of nineteenth-century missions to Africa. First, it will profile the perceptions of knowledge, intelligence and human abilities that existed in the period in which the translations under consideration were undertaken. This is the focus of Part I. Second, it will critically examine the historical accounts of the Efik New Testament translation project by Hugh Goldie in Old Calabar, Eastern Nigeria, and the Nyanja translation of Mark by Robert Laws at Livingstonia Mission, Central Africa. This is undertaken in Parts II and III. In Part IV, we consider developments since then.

The case for the Efik New Testament is made from secondary evidence related to the project. The case for the Nyanja translation is made from a close reading of Law's translation of Mark 1:1–8 in the light of the Third Edition of the UBS Greek New Testament, the translation of David Clement Scott, and that by the Union Nyanja Bible Translation Committee.

Part I

Background to Translation in the Nineteenth Century

1

An Overview of Bible Translation Theories from the Nineteenth Century to the Present

Introduction

Perceptions of the nature of biblical texts, target audiences and target Bible translations have been dominated by print-based theories from the dawn of Bible translation as mission in the Modern Missionary Movement[1] to the first half of the twenty-first century. This is largely because this period falls into the timeframe of affordable mass printing as well as a commonly held understanding that literacy went hand in hand with sophistication in thought and expression.

In this chapter, we briefly trace the history of Bible translation. We discuss the translation theories that governed Bible translation under the following periods: the Modern Missionary Movement; the United Bible Societies era; and the theories that have mushroomed following the challenge to theories of equivalence.

---

1. For the purposes of this book, the Modern Missionary Movement ranges from 1792–1992 in keeping with the periodization of a series dedicated to the movement. This period does not mark the beginning of Roman Catholic missions in Africa. W. R. Shenk, General Introduction to *Translation as Mission: Bible Translation in the Modern Missionary Movement*, The Modern Mission Era, 1792–1992: An Appraisal, by W. A. Smalley (Macon: Mercer University Press, 1991), ix.

The Modern Missionary Movement and Bible Translation

Bible translation has always been part of Christian mission and is not necessarily predicated on print culture.[2] However, current assumptions and practices in Bible translation in Africa, beginning with the poignantly named British and Foreign Bible Society (BFBS), later evolving into UBS (United Bible Societies), are products of the Modern Missionary Movement. The Bible Society movement began in 1804 and went on to become a major player in Bible translation: "The Bible Societies would not have been possible without printing, nor would the acceleration have been as great without the modern missionary movement which began at the same time."[3] Both the Bible Societies and the Modern Missionary Movement shared the vision to provide the Bible in the vernacular for people to read. They became the most important link between translators who were increasingly at work all over the world, and the printing press.[4]

The dominance of European thought and practices in the Modern Missionary Movement thrived because of the imperial expansionism of European nations of which it eventually became an integral part.[5] For instance, to a prominent Scottish missionary working at Livingstonia Mission Station in central Africa, mission education was a means of evangelizing people.[6]

Learning to read the Bible was thus both critical for securing the salvation of the natives, but also part of the larger agenda to bring Western civilization and skills to the natives. For this reason, missionaries were obligated to educate and evangelize without making any distinction between the two tasks. Consequently, mission schools were a source of skilled workers for both the mission and the colonial government.[7]

Missionaries of the Modern Missionary Movement largely shared the dominant perception at the end of the nineteenth century that there was only one culture: European culture. The indigenous people of the southern

---

2. J. A. Maxey, *From Orality to Orality: A New Paradigm for Contextual Translation of the Bible* (Eugene: Cascade Books, 2009), 19–20.

3. Smalley, 1991, 27.

4. Smalley, 1991, 27–28.

5. A. C. Ross, *Blantyre Mission and the Making of Modern Malawi* (Blantyre, Malawi: CLAIM, 1996), 129. Also see R. Oliver, *Sir Harry Johnston and the Scramble for Africa* (London: Chatto and Windus, 1957), 212.

6. R. Laws, *Reminiscences of Livingstonia* (Edinburgh: Oliver and Boyd, 1934), 176.

7. V. Chilenje, "The Origin and Development of the Church of Central Africa Presbyterian (CCAP) in Zambia," unpublished PhD Dissertation (Stellenbosch, South Africa: University of Stellenbosch, 2007), 140.

hemisphere did not possess culture. Therefore, mission to these peoples entailed bringing the gospel and culture.[8]

Missionaries translated the Bible into the vernacular languages of indigenous people, often first requiring reducing the language to writing, as part of evangelism. They then went ahead to perpetuate a textualized faith and to promote literacy in aid of the civilizing mandate.[9] According to Maxey, this continues to be the dominant rationale for Bible translation in the Bible Society movement to the present.[10] Lamin Sanneh argues, though, that translating the Bible into vernacular languages unleashed indigenous forces that were beyond the control of missionaries, leading to political as well as religious agency among Africans, as had been the case with Christian mission from its Judaic roots.[11]

Despite this commitment to translate into the vernacular, the rules of language that governed such Bible translation were presumed by the vast majority to be those evident in European languages, and a reflection of universal principles of grammar. Further, the civilizing mandate gave preference to European languages and culture.

For Ngugi Wa Thiong'o, language is representative of a people's culture and the enforced use of dominant colonizing languages was no less than the undermining of a people's identity.[12] And according to Bailey and Pippen, even translation as evangelism can be a tool for colonization if the ideological contributions of foreign translators are not identified and agency given to the indigenous peoples so that their ideological realities influence the translation.[13] For Sugirtharajah, an example of the inclusion of the ideological realities of target audiences for oral/aural cultures would be the privileging of "orality and the rhetoric of hearing" over written text.[14]

---

8. Maxey, *From Orality*, 21.

9. J. Comaroff and J. Comaroff, 1991, *Of Revelation and Revolution*, vol. 1. *Christianity, Colonialism, and Consciousness in South Africa* (Chicago: University of Chicago Press, 1991), 215.

10. Maxey, *From Orality*, 30.

11. L. Sanneh, *Translating the Message: The Missionary Impact on Culture* (Maryknoll: Orbis Books, 1989), 1, 17, 193.

12. N. wa Thiong'o, *Decolonizing the Mind: The Politics of Language in African Literature* (London: James Currey, 1986), 3.

13. R. C. Bailey and T. Pippen, eds., "Race, Class and the Politics of Biblical Translation," *Semeia* 76 (Atlanta: Scholars Press, 1996), 3.

14. R. S. Sugirtharajah, *Postcolonial Criticism and Biblical Interpretation* (Oxford: Oxford University Press, 2002), 56.

A History of Bible Translation in UBS Circles

Within UBS circles, Bible translation has been conducted under the rubric of the major theories that held sway at various times in Europe and the United States. Literal theories of translation first sought to translate the words and forms of respective source texts and only secondarily aimed to achieve clarity of their meanings.[15] Their guiding premise was that the very words of the source texts were the inspired conveyers of divine communication to target audiences. As such, their preservation through the adoption of literal equivalents in target texts was the critical task for translators.

Missionaries dominated Bible translation, often armed with knowledge of Hebrew, Greek and Latin and without an articulated translation theory other than the commitment to formal equivalence. Often influential European translations served alongside source language and Latin texts as source texts.[16]

Literal theories were followed by the dynamic equivalence theory whose most ardent advocate, and a revered figure in UBS circles, was Eugene Nida.[17] The genius of this theory lay in addressing the obvious challenge of finding literal equivalents in target texts for words and forms in source texts. This theory led to a shift towards aiming for meaning equivalence in the target texts instead of literal equivalence. This theory has dominated what Hermanson equates to the Bible Society Period, roughly from the mid-1960s to the present when several hitherto outposts of major European Bible societies attained autonomy.[18]

Subsequent Developments in Bible Translation Theory

Subsequently, several further questions and considerations have arisen. The presupposition that dynamic 'equivalence' can be attained has been challenged and several theories emerged that seek more realistic goals. In addition, the translation process itself has come under greater scrutiny leading to several translation theories.

Previously both literal and dynamic translation approaches upheld the priority of source texts and the imperative to transfer their meanings faithfully

---

15. J. S. Holmes, *Translated! Papers on Literary Translation and Translation Studies* (Amsterdam: Rodopi, 1988), 75.

16. E. A. Hermanson, "A Brief overview of Bible translation in South Africa," *Acta Theologica Supplementum* 2, 22.1 (2002): 7–8.

17. Nida's theory of Dynamic Equivalence is articulated in the definitive publication, E. A. Nida and C. A. Taber, *Theory and Practice of Translation* (Leiden, Brill, 2003).

18. Hermanson, "A Brief Overview," 9.

into target texts, a position that reflected the prominence of the Enlightenment ideal of the objective scholar who was able to execute his scholarly task without contributing any subjective realities of his own[19] and what Venuti calls "an instrumental model of translating."[20] Now the spotlight has been shone on the hitherto "invisible" translators and their contributions to the translating process. This focus on the inevitable contributions of translators appears as late as the 1980s.[21] Under this spotlight, translators are fully recognized as inevitable hermeneutists and their product invariably an interpretation.

This is in contrast to the prior understanding that translation is "the reproduction or transfer of an invariant contained in or caused by the source text, whether its form, its meaning, or its effect." Venuti labels this "a falsehood that cannot offer an incisive and comprehensive understanding of translation."[22] For him, two concepts define translation: (1) translation as an interpretative act; and (2) inscription, the turning of the source text into a translated text that is informed by the translating cultural difference.[23] In the end:

> Translation changes the form, meaning, and the effect of the source text, even when the translator maintains a semantic correspondence that creates a reliable basis for summaries and commentaries. Translation changes the cultural situation where the source text originated through the investment of prestige or the creation of stereotypes. Translation changes the receiving cultural situation by bringing into existence something new and different, a text that is neither the source text nor an original composition in the translating language, and in the process it changes the values, beliefs and representations that are housed in institutions.[24]

Another theory, Skopostheorie, highlighted the "goal of translation" (hence its *skopos*) as the key factor in determining the translator's construction of the target texts. This shifted the role of arbiter of what passes for a credible

---

19. B. Johnson, ed., *Freedom and Interpretation*, Oxford Amnesty Lectures (New York: Basic Books, 1993), 3.

20. L. Venuti, *Translation Changes Everything: Theory and Practice* (Abingdon, Oxon: Routledge, 2013), 3.

21. J. A. Naudé, "From Submissiveness to Agency: An overview of developments in translation studies and some implications for language practice in Africa," *Southern African Linguistics and Applied Language Studies*, 29.3 (2011): 223.

22. Venuti, *Translation*, 3.

23. Venuti, *Translation*, 4, 8.

24. Venuti, *Translation*, 10.

translation from the source text to the *skopos* of the translation as embodied in its translation brief. However, this also left the door open for unmitigated transformation of the source text by the translator.[25]

Functionalism borrows heavily from Skopostheorie in understanding the creative function of translators as inescapable; and the *skopos* of the translation as the key arbiter of the acceptability of a translation. For Nord, the ethical constraint of "loyalty" to the source text is adequate for achieving "similarity" with the source text.[26] This is because, after all, and especially in religious texts, the message is not subject to unmitigated reformulation. It is only subject to "retelling" to successive audiences and through different languages and media. With the advent of functionalism, translation studies have also moved away from the umbrella of applied and general linguistics, to a stand-alone discipline albeit in conversation with several other disciplines with which it is interrelated.[27]

This development has also meant a re-evaluation of the nature of the biblical texts. Whereas literary scholars traditionally focused on genre in their analysis and viewed the sentence as the key conveyer of meaning,[28] translation studies now consider communication as the governing principle and the text as a whole – as well as realities beyond the text – as part of the communicative praxis between communicator and recipient of communication. This conversation has taken place as culturally defined "frames of reference."

Performance criticism is an extension of functionalism due to a fresh understanding of the biblical texts as relics of functional oral performances. Each performance is presumed to have had a specific target audience and was shaped to achieve communication. As such, the dynamics that govern oral/aural communication should be presumed to be responsible for the form and function of the biblical texts, not those that govern literature in the context of a print culture.[29]

---

25. C. Nord, "Functionalist Approaches," in Y. Gambier & L. Van Doorslaer, eds., *Handbook of Translation Studies*, vol. 1 (Amsterdam/Philadelphia: John Benjamins, 2010), 8.

26. Nord, "Functionalist Approaches," 8.

27. J. A. Naudé, "An Overview of Recent developments in Translation Studies with Special Reference to the Implications for Bible Translation," *Acta Theologica Supplementum* 2 (2002): 44-45.

28. Holmes, *Translated!*, 75.

29. D. Rhoads, "What is Performance Criticism?" in H. E. Hearon and P. Ruge-Jones, eds., *The Bible in Ancient and Modern Media: Story and Performance* (Eugene: Cascade Books, 2009), 83.

According to De Vries, this trajectory of research demands a re-evaluation of two tasks related to Bible translation: (1) the way we understand the texts (the exegetical task); and (2) the way we may translate the Bible differently if the target audience of a translation shares the same propensity for orality that most of the biblical audiences evidenced (the translation task).[30] Ongoing research into the nature of orality and its interface with textuality has shown that both orality and literacy are equally capable of abstract logic and that the oral-written continuum is not a sustainable thesis. Research has also shown that orality and writing were not mutually exclusive but intimately connected and worked together.[31]

A significant quantity of Bible translations into vernacular languages in Africa is for target audiences that encounter the Bible as performance (whether through public readings or homilies) due to very high levels of illiteracy. As such, paratextual elements that target hearing, as opposed to those that target reading (and therefore, the eye), must be understood and deliberately incorporated in such translations in aid of communication and comprehension.[32] This is still preferable although, as Makutoane et al. note, orality is not homogenous.[33] As such the quest to translate the oral features in the source language texts for an oral target audience is a complicated matter.

In actual practice in Bible translation in Africa, Nida's dynamic equivalence theory is the dominant theory in UBS circles. In addition, a key UBS policy is to serve all the churches that are part of the fellowship. This means that "the respective understanding of language and translation and Scripture" of a given church overrides any other considerations in specific projects.[34] Such understandings are typically made clear in a project's Translation Brief, the key document that spells out the nature of a project, and the translation theory to be employed.

---

30. L. De Vries, "Local Oral-Written Interfaces and Nature, Transmission, Performance, and Translation of Biblical Texts," in J. A. Maxey and E. R. Wendland, eds., *Translating Scripture for Performance: New Directions in Biblical Studies* (Eugene: Cascade Books, 2012), 69.

31. De Vries, "Local Interfaces," 89.

32. De Vries, "Local Interfaces," 79.

33. Makotoane, et al., "Similarity and alterity in translating the orality of the Old Testament in oral cultures," *Translation Studies* 8.2 (2015): 156.

34. P. A. Noss, "Current Trends in Scripture Translation," in P. A. Noss, ed., *Current Trends in Scripture Translation*, Bulletin Number 194/195 (Reading, UK: United Bible Societies, 2002), 4.

2

The Enlightenment, Mission and Imperialism

In order to identify and evaluate the epistemological framework in which the Modern Missionary Movement operated in a fair and accurate manner, it is necessary to situate this framework in a larger one, namely, the political, economic and philosophical theories of the time. It is also necessary to estimate, based on historical accounts, how much this epistemological framework influenced the theory and practice of the missionary organizations and personnel of the era.

In this book, we will associate the Modern Missionary Movement with the period 1792–1992 in keeping with the parameters set by *Translation as Mission*, a series dedicated to appraising the movement.[1] However, the translations that we will consider only extend to 1922. Shenk represents majority opinion in citing the Enlightenment as the most important development of the eighteenth century, "a powerful constellation of fresh ideas that released forces affecting all areas of human existence and inexorably extended to all parts of the globe."[2]

The Enlightenment was a European phenomenon and fostered in Europeans a new spirit and outlook. It was carried along by a dynamic "Western messianism" and, by the end of the eighteenth century, had been translated into a political program based on liberal, democratic and nationalist ideas.[3]

For Lesslie Newbigin, the onset and proliferation of the Enlightenment amounted to transferring the holy city from an eschatological, otherworldly

---

1. Shenk, General Introduction to *Translation as Mission*, ix. As will become evident, this period does not mark the beginning of Roman Catholic missions in Africa.
2. Shenk, General Introduction, x.
3. Shenk, General Introduction, x.

dimension to this world.⁴ Accordingly, "the eighteenth century witnessed the birth of the doctrine of progress, a doctrine that was the rule – with fateful consequences – well into the twentieth century."⁵

Through its doctrine of the powers and possibilities of human reason and an attitude of radical skepticism, the Enlightenment posed intense and aggressive challenges to religion.⁶ However, from a broader perspective, the Enlightenment era was still a part of the Hellenic-European phase of epistemological dominion that lasted well into the twentieth century. Under this phase, Europe became the geographical heartland of Christianity and the Christian expansion that ensued was almost exclusively a European expression of Christianity.⁷

A fundamental element of modernity has been the division of human life into public and private, and the separation of fact and value.⁸ In general, the Western concept of culture has consequently promoted critical distrust of religion.⁹ More importantly in the broader perspective, modernity launched modern man on his path to exploration and conquest of unknown frontiers both in the epistemological and physical senses.

It must be pointed out, however, that the Modern Missionary Movement as an expansionist organization preceded imperialist expansion and was inspired by mission-related motives. This is mission as the biblical command to facilitate "a passage over the boundary between faith in Jesus Christ and its absence" for every human being on the face of the earth.¹⁰ When imperialist expansionism eventually caught up and joined forces with the Modern Missionary Movement, it was as two separate movements that shared substantial common interests and goals.

---

4. Newbigin argues that "the medieval Christian, taught by the Bible, saw as an end to which all history moves, the second coming of Christ, the judgement of living and dead, and the holy city in which all that is pure and true in the public and private life of nations is gathered up in eternal perfection. This vision of the end is, of course, part and parcel of the teleological view of creation and history, which has the will and purpose of God at its centre." *Foolishness to the Greeks: The Gospel and Western Culture* (Geneva: World Council of Churches; Grand Rapids: Eerdmans, 1986), 28, 34.

5. Newbigin, *Foolishness to the Greeks*, 34.

6. Shenk, General Introduction, x.

7. Shenk, General Introduction, xi.

8. Newbigin, *Foolishness to the Greeks*, 34.

9. L. Sanneh, *Encountering the West. Christianity and the Global Cultural Process: The African Dimension* (London: Marshall Pickering, 1993), 29.

10. Sanneh, *Translating the Message*, xi.

A case in point is David Livingstone (1813–1873) whose incursions into the interior of central Africa inspired the setting up of two missionary societies in the area[11] and a British Protectorate. Livingstone's agenda was to transform African society through commerce and Christianity. He held that the barriers preventing the new life that the gospel brings from coming to fruition in Africa were the actual structures of African society. This fundamentally included the slave trade.[12]

It is with this "Livingstonian" understanding of mission that the Free Church pioneers came to Malawi. It is also in the interest of this philosophy of mission that in the 1880s Scottish Missions built up enough support in Scotland to put pressure on the British Government to declare a Protectorate after threats in the 1880s that the Shire Highlands might become Portuguese territory. Apparently, the fear accompanying this request was that a territorial takeover by the more exploitative Portuguese was not in the African's interest.[13]

This theory of mission was also held by D. C. Scott, perhaps the most significant and idealistically progressive missionary of the Blantyre Mission, and fully committed to bearing both the gospel and modern culture to Africa. He differed with many of his colleagues at Blantyre Mission and in the Modern Missionary Movement in holding convictions that saw Africans as human beings who were essentially not different from Europeans. He also saw them as ready for responsibility both in the church and in the new society created in Africa by the coming of European power.[14] However, these views were held from a civilizing agenda:

> The culture brought by the missionaries was not, he believed, simply European culture but a modern culture, world-wide in its significance. He insisted that Africans were its inheritors as much as Europeans . . . Scott held that since Africans were co-inheritors of modern culture, it should be imparted consciously in

---

11. The Free Church of Scotland set up Livingstonia Mission initially based at Cape Maclear on the shores of modern Lake Malawi. The name Livingstonia was derived from David Livingstone's surname. H. McIntosh, *Robert Laws: Servant of Africa* (The Stables, Carberry, Scotland: The Handsel Press Ltd., 1993), 13. The Established Church of Scotland set Blantyre Mission in the same area at about the same time. Blantyre is the name of David Livingstone's birthplace. Ross, *Blantyre Mission*, 15–16; McIntosh, *Robert Laws*, 49. Also see K. J. McCracken, *Politics and Christianity in Malawi: 1875–1940* (Cambridge: Cambridge University Press, 1977).

12. Ross, *Blantyre Mission*, 16. "He believed that a legitimate European commercial presence could, when backed by the educational as well as evangelistic influence of Christian mission, set Africa free to find a new future."

13. Ross, *Blantyre Mission*, 14.

14. Ross, *Blantyre Mission*, 63, 65.

the educational process hoping that as with the Gospel, it would ground itself in African forms.[15]

Ironically, in advocating for a deliberate civilizing and modernizing role, Scott was exhibiting a more sympathetic view for the African and was, in essence, digressing from the expectations of his superiors in Scotland, although he was fulfilling the vision of David Livingstone. Inherent in Scott's and, before him, Livingstone's philosophies of mission, was the often unexpressed acceptance in missionary circles and beyond that Africans, in spite of their ontological equality with Europeans, were intellectually underdeveloped and existentially backward. This is what transformed the civilizing mandate from an unwarranted hegemony into a humane and "Christian" project.

In contrast, as part of the recommendations of an inquiry following the Blantyre Crisis[16] that immediately preceded the coming of Scott to Blantyre Mission, Thomas Pringle had explicitly refused to accept the missionary as having any civilizing role to play. His argument was that successful evangelization could take place apart from any great cultural change among African people.[17] However, while purporting to represent an attitude that respected African culture, unlike the very prevalent missionary attitude of aversion to all things African, his position likely masked the growing understanding that Africans were incapable of becoming civilized. This would be in agreement with the increasingly popular social evolutionary theory that placed Africans close to the bottom of the human evolutionary scale.[18] It probably also masked a distaste

---

15. Ross, *Blantyre Mission*, 63.

16. The Blantyre Crisis refers to the unmitigated judicial practices of Blantyre Mission personnel towards native Africans that preceded the era of D. C. Scott. "The controversy was made public in Britain when an Australian hunter and traveller, Andrew Chirnside, who had been in the area when some of the incidents took place, published a pamphlet in 1880, *The Blantyre Missionaries: Discreditable Disclosures* J. Thompson, *Touching the Heart: Xhosa Missionaries to Malawi, 1876–1888*, African Initiatives in Christian Mission 5 (Pretoria: University of South Africa, 2000), 69. See pages 68–73 for a fuller account.

17. The care of the sick was equally not an essential part of the gospel but a subordinate adjunct to the work of evangelization. Assembly Reports, 1881, FMC Report, Appendix A. For the widespread nature of this view in the church circles of Scotland, see H. A. C. Cairns, *Prelude to Imperialism: British Reaction to Central African Society 1840–1890* (London: Routledge & Kegan Paul, 1965), 219.

18. H. Johnston, *The Backward Peoples and Our Relations with Them* (London, New York, Melbourne, Cape Town, Bombay, Calcutta, Madras, Shanghai, Peking, Copenhagen: Oxford University Press, 1920), 7, 36. Also see A. F. Walls, "Samuel Ajayi Crowther 1807–1891: Foremost African Christian of the Nineteenth Century," in *Mission Legacies: Biographical Studies of Leaders of the Modern Missionary Movement* (Maryknoll: Orbis Books, 1994), 264.

which existed even at this early date for Africans who "aped" the European in such matters as clothing.[19]

Scott's judgement about the desirability of civilizing the African was shared by the vast majority of Africans who were more than happy to discard their Africanness for the promise of becoming like their European masters.[20] However, when the British Government eventually made the area a Protectorate, it was not because of an optimistic view of the African. It was partly a recapitulation to the pressure in Scotland for the safety of the British missionary staff in the area.[21] It was also for possible exploitative interests. For example, it was the view of the first British Commissioner for the Area, Sir Harry Johnston, that the white man carried the burden of responsibility for the total wellbeing of the heathen, and that this burden included the obligation to take over the African's resources and freedoms for his or her numerical preservation and betterment. This burden included the exploitation of Africa's natural resources for the benefit of the civilized world.[22]

The era of imperial expansion coincided with social Darwinism in Europe and that theory was soon influencing mission policy and practice.[23] Ross makes the claim that the older "industrial mission" view of mission prevailed much longer in Scottish missions, surviving well into the mid-nineties.[24] But this could be attributed more to the convictions and resilience of individual missionary figures like D. C. Scott rather than to popular sentiment among the policy-makers in Scotland. With the departure of Scott from Blantyre Mission and despite the efforts of his successor, Hetherwick, to maintain the tradition of Scott, the gap between missionary and native widened. Mission was now part of the imperial establishment and the role that it now came to play was one of striving to correct specific injustices from within the establishment.[25]

Thus, at the turn of the twentieth century, we find hegemony perpetuated by imperialism and mission for different reasons, but sharing the same low estimation of the African. Initially a term referring to the dominance of one

---

19. Cairns, *Prelude to Imperialism*, 221.

20. J. Booth, *Africa for the African*, ed. Laura Perry (Blantyre, Malawi: CLAIM, 1996), 18–19.

21. Ross, *Blantyre Mission*, 14, 25, 84, 85–88, 92.

22. Johnston, *The Backward Peoples*, 42, 56, 59.

23. J. F. A. Ajayi, *Christian Missions in Nigeria, 1841–1891: The Making of a New Élite* (London: Longmans, Green and Co. Ltd., 1965), 233–73.

24. *Blantyre Mission*, 118.

25. Ross, *Blantyre Mission*, 129. Also see R. Oliver, *Sir Harry Johnston and the Scramble for Africa* (London: Chatto and Windus, 1957), 212.

state within a confederation, hegemony is now generally understood to mean domination by consent:

> This broader meaning was coined and popularized in the 1930s by Italian Marxist Antonio Gramci, who investigated why the ruling class was so successful in promoting its own interests in society. Fundamentally, hegemony is the power of the ruling class to convince other classes that their interests are the interests of all. Domination is thus exerted not by force, nor even necessarily by active persuasion, but by a more subtle and inclusive power over the economy, and over state apparatuses such as education and the media, by which the ruling class's interest is presented as the common interest and thus comes to be taken for granted. The term is useful for describing the success of imperial power over a colonised people who may outnumber any occupying military force but whose desire for self-determination has been suppressed by a hegemonic notion of the greater good, often couched in terms of social order, stability and advancement, all of which are defined by the colonising power.[26]

Hegemony in Africa persisted well into the twentieth century and even beyond the twentieth century. For example, Ngugi Wa Thiong'o has argued forcefully that the perpetuation of the hegemony of Western patterns of thought, policies, administrative practices and civic structures is encouraged and enforced by the politically independent but ideologically colonized post-colonial African bureaucrats and aristocrats who are products and disciples of the very hegemony that they professed to overthrow with the attainment of political independence.[27]

In the course of the evolution of imperial interests, the fortunes of European hegemony changed in keeping with the rising consciousness of ontological equality in Africans that has, largely and paradoxically, been attributed to the success of the Modern Missionary Movement in both its Christianizing and civilizing endeavours. Ross, for example, credits the Blantyre Mission and the Livingstonia Mission to the north with being "the seedbed of the nationalist

---

26. B. Ashcroft, Gareth Griffiths and Helen Tifin, *Key Concepts in Post-Colonial Studies* (London and New York: Routledge, 1998), 116.

27. *Homecoming: Essays on African and Caribbean Literature, Culture and Politics* (London: Heinemann, 1972), 36; and N. Wa Thiong'o, *Decolonising the Mind*, 4.

movement which finally succeeded in achieving independence for Malawi in 1964."²⁸

This paradox is, interestingly, acknowledged even by those who are inclined to let the spotlight rest on the overwhelming evidence of the overt repression and denigration of African cultures and consciousness by European missionaries and colonists.²⁹ It is argued that, in spite of this repression and denigration, the message of human equality inherent in the gospel had penetrated deep enough to spawn an African consciousness that subverted this hegemony.

For Sanneh, the ultimate instrument for this subversion was the Bible translation machinery that the Modern Missionary Movement put in place as, perhaps, the one task that was viewed as a priority by mission organizations across the board. Reading the Bible in their languages both enhanced the Africans' access to its message, thereby diminishing the role of the missionary as spiritual guide and expositor of the Scriptures, and elevated the vernacular languages and, by extension, African cultures into legitimate revelatory media of God's sacred message.³⁰

As a result of this rise in consciousness, the decade immediately following the middle of the twentieth century witnessed the attainment of political independence by the vast majority of European colonies in Africa. Yet, when hegemony is primarily understood as "the capacity to influence the thought of the colonized, where consent is achieved by the interpellation of the colonized subject by imperial discourse so that Eurocentric values, assumptions, beliefs and attitudes are accepted as a matter of course as the most natural and valuable,"³¹ Africa is still under European hegemony.

However, some, such as Sanneh, argue that this is an inaccurate assessment of the effects of the Modern Missionary Movement. This is because it pays insufficient attention to the subversive influences released by the Modern

---

28. *Blantyre Mission*, 13. See also A. Hastings, *A History of African Christianity 1950–1975* (Cambridge: Cambridge University Press, 1976), 10–12. See K. N. Mufuka, *Missions and Politics in Malawi* (Kingston, Ontario: The Limestone Press, 1977), 146–95, for a Malawian voice with similar views.

29. F. B. Welbourn and B. A. Ogot, *A Place to Feel at Home: A Story of Two Independent Churches in Western Kenya* (London: Oxford University Press, 1966), 33, 133–34; J. V. Taylor, *The Growth of the Church in Buganda* (London: S.C.M. Press, 1958), 42; L. J. Luzbetak, *The Church and Cultures: New Perspectives in Missiological Anthropology* (Maryknoll: Orbis Books, 1988), 68.

30. Sanneh, *Translating the Message*, 4, 62, 173, 188. Also see R. Oliver, *The Missionary Factor in East Africa* (London: Longman, 1952; rep. 1970), 184.

31. Ashcroft, Griffiths and Tifin, *Key Concepts in Post-Colonial Studies*, 117.

Missionary Movement that facilitated the rediscovery of African agency in African institutions.[32] Nevertheless, as I have argued elsewhere, in his desire to champion African agency in the midst of undeniable European hegemony, Sanneh has overlooked the glaring perpetuation of Eurocentric values, assumptions, beliefs, and attitudes by the very Africans that he credits agency with or, at the very least, the real power-brokers and policy-makers in Africa.[33]

European hegemony came with its own epistemological theories, practice and politics that gave rise to specific theories of language and translation in the mission field. In the context of Russia, for example, Stephen K. Batalden notes that modern biblical translations arise out of particular political and cultural contexts. In addition, since translations are products of one or another political culture, paying close attention to the politics of biblical translation can illumine broader issues in the relationship between church and society.[34]

Enlightenment ideas elevated the place of human reason and a radical skepticism that demanded careful investigation, through predominantly rational processes, in epistemology. The resultant "scientific" method and its protégé, science, were understood as the sole arbiters of knowledge by virtue of holding the keys to inviolable "scientific" laws to which all branches of human knowledge had to answer.[35] With this understanding came the theory that "Grammar is the science of words and the art of employing words according to the established usage of a Language," and that "the leading Principles of Grammar must necessarily be the same in all Languages."[36] Consequently, up until about eighty years ago, a good knowledge of the biblical languages and of exegetical methods and findings was regarded as sufficient qualification for translating the Bible.[37] The use of native speakers as respondents to the

---

32. Sanneh, *Translating the Message*, 172–73, 188. Also see Smalley, *Translation as Mission*, xii.

33. M. Nyirenda, "Epistemological Hegemony in the History of Christianity in Africa and the Question of Translatability in the Light of the Thesis of Lamin Sanneh in *Translating the Message*," MTh. (R) Paper I, CSCNWW, University of Edinburgh, 2001.

34. "The Politics of Modern Russian Biblical Translation," in *Bible Translation and the Spread of the Church: The Last 200 Years*, ed. Philip C. Stine (Leiden: Brill, 1990), 68.

35. Smalley, *Translation as Mission*, x.

36. H. Goldie, *Principles of Efik Grammar: with Specimen of the Language* (Edinburgh: Muir and Paterson, 1868), 13. Quoting Goldie here illustrates how directly Enlightenment theory translated into actual translation practice on the mission field. It must not be surmised, however, that every missionary subscribed to this theory of grammar.

37. P. C. Stine, Introduction to *Bible Translation and the Spread of the Church*, vii.

missionary's questions usually sufficed as a basis for reducing native languages to writing and translating the Bible into those languages.[38]

In contrast to Enlightenment thought, African rationality and spirituality are rooted in holism. Holism may be defined as the phenomenon of seeing individual units in the context of the whole they belong to.[39] This is the opposite of the polarization inherent in Enlightenment epistemology: public and private; fact and value; secular and sacred; intellect and emotion; fact and theory; etc. Holism permeates everything in African epistemology – the secular is sacred and the material is spiritual.[40] The individual's identity is in the group's identity.[41] Abstract rationality is inextricably intertwined with the senses and the emotions.[42] Time is understood as event. This means that time is primarily conceptualized together with *what* happens as opposed to a *when* it happens that is independent of the activity.[43]

In epistemological method, holism means that grasping the whole precedes and governs understanding the particular.[44] In language theory, this means that the philosophy behind etymology and epistemological context, not inviolable rules, govern phonology, grammar and syntax.[45] It is also for this reason that

---

38. Smalley, *Translation as Mission*, 15.

39. D. M. Gitari and G. P. Benson, eds., *Witnessing to the Living God in Contemporary Africa* (Nairobi: African Theological Fraternity, 1986), vii.

40. J. S. Mbiti, *The Prayers of African Religion* (Maryknoll: Orbis Books, 1975), 2. Also see M. Mead, *Growing Up in New Guinea* (New York: Mentor Books, 1953), 67.

41. S. Nomenyo, "Theology in the Life of the Churches," in *African Challenge*, edited by Kenneth Y. Best (Nairobi, Kenya: Transafrica Publishers, 1975), 71, 73; K. A. Dickson, *Theology in Africa* (London: Darton Longman and Todd; Maryknoll: Orbis Books, 1984), 62; S. Sidhom, "The Theological Estimate of Man," in *Biblical Revelation and African Beliefs*, edited by K. A. Dickson and P. Ellingworth (London: Lutterworth Press, 1969), 99, 102; J. S. Mbiti, *The Study of African Religion & Philosophy* (London: Heinemann, 1969), 104–5.

42. G. O. West, *Biblical Hermeneutics of Liberation*, 2nd rev. ed. (Maryknoll: Orbis Books, 1995), 85; D. C. Scott, *A Cyclopaedic Dictionary of the Mang'anja Language spoken in British Central Africa* (Edinburgh: The Foreign Mission Committee for the Church of Scotland, 1862), xxii.

43. See J. S. Mbiti, *New Testament Eschatology in an African Background* (London: Oxford University Press, 1971), 24; Mbiti, *African Religions & Philosophy*, 19; J. Parrat, "Time in Traditional African Thought," *Religion* 7 (1977), 118.

44. See the resolutions of the All Africa Conference of Churches (AACC), Abidjan, September 1969. See also F. D. E. Schleiermacher, *Hermeneutics: The Hand-written Manuscripts*, edited by H. Kimmerle (Missioula: Scholars Press, 1977), 168.

45. See D. Tarr, *Double Image: Biblical Insights from African Parables* (New York and Mahwah: Paulist Press, 1984), 153.

dramatic re-enactment, otherwise called "narrative" or "storytelling," is of the essence of African communication.[46]

It was not until Eugene A. Nida joined the American Bible Society staff in 1943 that the promotion of professional expertise, the development of translation theory and of procedures based on such theory, began.[47] "Up to that time, the Bible societies[48] had given what advice they could to translators, and had sought to ensure the value and quality of each translation as well as they knew how, but had not developed an articulated theoretical base."[49]

In all these areas, Nida and the new breed of Bible translators incorporated work from a number of fields including linguistics, socio-linguistics and cultural anthropology, cognitive science and psychology, communication science, semiotics, and literary criticism. These considerations are producing translators that are more open and receptive to cultural, sociological and psychological dynamics in the churches and societies where they are working.[50]

In the absence of a developed and articulated theoretical base for translation, translators tended to resort to what they knew about language which, in most cases, meant what they themselves had learned. For many, this meant a strong classical education in the style of the times with years of Latin and Greek study in secondary school, university, and seminary.[51] "Folk" theories of translation, unsystematic ideas about how translation should be done, existed nevertheless. One source of such translation folk theory was contemporary language instruction predicated on lexical and grammatical matching:

> Professors often tested students by requiring them to translate a passage from the language they were studying. The aim was to show in their own language, as much as they could of the

---

46. See P. B. Hammond, ed., *Cultural and Social Anthropology: Selected Readings* (New York: The Macmillan Company, 1964), 364.

47. Smalley, *Translation as Mission*, 28. Cf. E. M. North, "Eugene A. Nida: An Appreciation," in *Language, Culture and Religion: In Honor of Eugene A. Nida*, Matthew Black and William A. Smalley, eds. (The Hague: Mouton, 1974), vii–xx.

48. The Bible Society movement began in 1804 and went on to become a major player in Bible translation. "The Bible Societies would not have been possible without printing, nor would the acceleration have been as great without the modern missionary movement which began at the same time." Both the Bible Societies and the Modern Missionary Movement shared the vision to provide the Bible in the vernaculars for people to read. They became the most important link between translators who were increasingly at work all over the world, and the printing press. They were also a source of financial assistance. Smalley, *Translation as Mission*, 27–28.

49. Smalley, *Translation as Mission*, 28.

50. Stine, Introduction to *Bible Translation and the Spread of the Church*, vii.

51. Smalley, *Translation as Mission*, 105, 106.

grammatical structure and the meanings of the words in the text from which they were translating. They were to provide a fairly close receptor language match for each source language word and for each grammatical structure so that the professor could see that they knew the word, and that they recognized the grammatical structures of the text.[52]

It is not surprising, then, that direct correspondence between words and grammatical structures, rather than dynamic equivalence, was the predominant approach to translation.

Nida, perhaps the most important person in the formulation of dynamic equivalence translation (or functional equivalence as he later called it), contrasts the theory with formal correspondence by which he means literal translation. A literal translation:

> Matches or corresponds to the original in various formal, surface ways, but gives the wrong meaning or obscures the meaning or renders the communication awkward and unnatural. In dynamic equivalence translation, meaning and impact in the receptor, the reader or hearer of the translation should be as close as possible to the meaning and impact which the message had for the original receptors.[53]

The point is well made, however, that, in most cases, availability and desire to be involved proved to be the determining factor in the selection of translators. As Smalley noted with respect to Modern Missionary Movement Bible translators,

> People do not normally become missionaries in order to be Bible translators. They enlist as pastors, teachers, even agriculturists, doctors or nurses; but in time some are selected to become translators because translation is needed, and there is nobody

---

52. E. Torre, "My First Attempts at Translating," *The Jerome Quarterly* 4 (1989): 8.

53. Smalley, *Translation as Mission*, 111. See also J. deWard and E. A. Nida, *From One Language to Another: Functional Equivalence in Bible Translating* (Nashville: Thomas Nelson, 1986), vii; M. L. Larson, *Meaning-Based Translation: A Guide to Cross-Language Equivalence* (Lanham: University of America, 1984); J. Beekman and John Callow, *Translating the Word of God* (Grand Rapids: Zondervan, 1974).

else to do it. So Bible translators are sometimes a motley crew when matched against ideal criteria.[54]

In fact, one is hard-pressed to find a Bible translator in the Modern Missionary Movement who is not acutely aware of their limitations as translators and the tentative nature of their works.[55]

However, just as the acceptability and popularity of various translations has differed over the years,[56] so with the translations done within the Modern Missionary Movement. Smalley notes that it is possible for a translation, by virtue of its popularity and acceptability, to exceed, in influence and authority, texts in the original languages to the extent that subsequent translations are generally made from it in preference to making them from texts in original languages. His examples include Jerome's AD 405 Latin Vulgate that became the standard Bible of Roman Catholic Christianity for over a thousand years. Or, before it, the Greek Septuagint that became the primary text upon which Old Testament translations were made. Some Modern Missionary Movement first translations wield similar power and influence:

> Traditionally, missionary translators were very powerful people . . . They were very powerful because they decided what the Bible meant, and watched to see that the meaning they understood was the one conveyed to a whole church. They were the gatekeepers of truth.[57]

These sometimes reflected the power and influence of missionaries in the Bible translation process:

> If anyone on the translation team knew the original languages, they did, or at least they were the ones who had access to the commentaries and to other translations to help them. They

---

54. Smalley, *Translation as Mission*, 16. Smalley is writing with respect to the selection criteria of the ideologically conscious translation projects conducted by the Summer Institute of Linguistics. It does not take much imagination to approximate how much more eclectic and ill prepared were the translators before Bible translation was a professional undertaking with a clear and informed translation theory. For an example see Thompson, *Touching the Heart*, 89–90; see also 81–82.

55. For examples see R. F. Young, *Resistant Hinduism: Sanskrit Sources on Anti-Christian Apologetics in Early 19th Century India*, Nobili Research Library 8 (Vienna: Institut für Indeologie der Universität Wien, 1981), 35, on William Carey (1761–1834) and his self-perception of the translations that he did; and Hugh Goldie's prefatory note to his translation of the *Efik New Testament* (Edinburgh: Murray Ye Gibb, 1862), 2.

56. Smalley, *Translation as Mission*, 24.

57. Smalley, *Translation as Mission*, 224.

could stop any argument, quell any uneasiness about awkward or misleading wording in the translation by insisting that "that is what the Greek says!"[58]

In other cases, it was the cultural status that some translations attained that established their authority and influence, as in the case of the King James Version of 1611.[59]

These examples demonstrate that the acceptability and popularity of a translation does not always correspond to the quality of the translation. However, in the light of today's superior understanding of translation theory as attempted accessibility, it remains the challenge of translators to constantly re-evaluate the quality of their translations in order to arrive at better quality work in both future revisions and new translations of the Bible.

Accessibility recognizes that translators have to cope with vast time and cultural distance, incompatibility of literary styles (if any), and greater differences in linguistic structure. It also understands the translator as one who is trying to gain access into two worlds of meaning: that of the biblical texts as message to be translated and that of the target language.

In the light of these challenges, accessibility recognizes that perfect translation is impossible because no two languages are the same, no two cultures are the same, and the world view of no two people is the same. Therefore, translation is always an approximation of the original: "some degree of accessibility and distortion are therefore the anticipated product and inevitable byproduct of all translation. The skilful translator seeks to maximize accessibility and minimize distortion of all kinds, but skewing can never be absolutely eliminated."[60] It is for this reason that the deconstructive review of the two translation projects in Part II is also a basis for constructive work in the form of future revisions.

---

58. Smalley, *Translation as Mission*, 224.

59. Smalley, *Translation as Mission*, 18. Smalley goes on to note that the King James Version of the Bible has continued to enjoy massive use in spite of the now well-known fact that its translators used later manuscripts than were at the disposal of the Bible translators of the twentieth century and in spite of the antiquated nature of the English that it was translated into.

60. Smalley, *Translation as Mission*, 3.

Part II

The Efik New Testament Bible Translation

3

The Historical Forces behind the Old Calabar Mission

Chapter 2 gave a summary of the state of epistemological theory in the Modern Missionary Movement in the context of the political, economic and philosophical theories of the day. In this chapter, we will review a segment of this period from the perspective of the forces in history that gave rise to and shaped the Old Calabar Mission in general and the translation of the Efik New Testament in particular.

To shed some light on the world in which the Rev. Hugh Goldie produced his translation of the Efik New Testament, we will attempt to establish two things. First, we examine the circumstances of the establishment of the Old Calabar Mission.[1] Second, we will determine, as much as possible, the values, judgements and aspirations of those who were closely associated with the story of this mission both locally and abroad.

Because of the interest that this mission generated in Scotland, we may safely extrapolate that when a minister of the United Presbyterian Church writes about the Old Calabar Mission barely four decades from the unfolding of the story itself,[2] he is representing sentiments and perceptions that are

---

1. Apparently, "the native name is Efik. There is a New Calabar, reached through a creek off the Ibanni (Bonny) branch of the Niger. This was probably a settlement from Calabar, Now called Old for the sake of distinction." H. Goldie, *Calabar and its Mission: with additional chapters by Rev. John Taylor Dean* (Edinburgh and London: Oliphant, Anderson & Ferrier, 1901), 9, note 1.

2. The Rev. William Dickie confesses in the preface to his book that his aim was not to supply a history of "our mission in Old Calabar." Rather, his account is "a labour of love," confirming his convictions that missions are the lifeblood of the church and the inspiration of every vital ministry. The account is also meant to recapture the strife and heroism and triumphs associated with the earlier years of "our work on the western shores of Africa" for posterity. *Story of the Mission in Old Calabar*, Missions of the United Presbyterian Church (Edinburgh: Offices of United Presbyterian Church, 1894), 5–6.

not unique to himself. Goldie records that when the emissary of the Jamaica Presbytery, Rev. H. M. Waddell, was granted permission from the directors of the Scottish Missionary Society to go to Scotland to lay the scheme of the new mission before the churches, he generated immense interest in the people:

> The romance associated with it, – a mission into a then unknown region, far apart from any European settlements, and which had been one of the principal seats of the slave trade, together with sympathy for desolated Africa, – drew forth the warm hopes and aid of many who had not formerly given their sympathy to mission effort. The interest was necessarily greatest in the denomination which had adopted it, being of unmitigated heathenism, and the zeal which it excited gave an impetus to the missionary effort of the whole of the Scottish Churches.[3]

When the Modern Missionary Movement proclaimed Christianity along the West Coast of Africa, it was not introducing a novel faith. According to J. B. Grimley and Gordon E. Robinson, "evidence in some of the ancient art forms indicates that Christianity was known many centuries ago."[4] Some historians speculate that immigrants from the Mediterranean area, who brought the Coptic or some other form of Christianity along with them, originally settled in Nigeria. In time, they assume that this Christianity died out and was swallowed up by animistic religious beliefs.[5]

Therefore, when the Modern Missionary Movement arrived in this area, it was most likely re-introducing a familiar message but now within an Indo-European epistemological frame. Moreover, between the advent of Modern Missions and the earlier presence of Christianity in Africa, there already was a failed attempt to reach Southern Nigeria by Roman Catholic missionaries: "As far back as 1487 Portuguese missionaries laboured in Benin City and in what is now called Old Warri. Owing to climatic conditions and two wars in Europe their missionary work was discontinued and their converts lapsed into paganism."[6]

However, according to Ajayi, the root cause of this mission's demise, whose protagonists he identifies more specifically as Spanish, Italian and Portuguese

---

3. *Calabar and its Mission*, 76–77.

4. J. B. Grimley and G. E. Robinson, *Church Growth in Central and Southern Nigeria* (Grand Rapids: Eerdmans, 1966), 269.

5. Grimley and Robinson, *Church Growth in Central and Southern Nigeria*, 269.

6. *The Nigeria Catholic Directory* (Yaba, Nigeria: National Office, 1962), 68.

Roman Catholics, was in the failure by its missionaries to comprehend the holistic nature of the African world view:

> To the people of Benin and Warri religion meant one thing, and to their Christian teachers quite another thing . . . To a people for whom religion was co-extensive with life, the Europeans presented trade and religion as two separate institutions, championed by two separate sets of people and guided by two different sets of principles. The missionaries were dependent on the traders for their transport and provisions, but they could not convincingly reconcile their teaching with the Atlantic slave trade and slavery as practised in the New World. . . . Thus the missionaries concentrated only on the aspect of personal belief and forms of worship and consequently paid inadequate attention to education. For that reason, they failed to understand the society they were dealing with. They saw in traditional religion no more than fetishes, idolatry, and juju.[7]

Apparently, the failure by the Roman Catholic missionaries to appreciate the central and all-pervasive role of religion for the stability and self-awareness of African societies meant that the missionaries lacked the ability to effect deep-seated and lasting change. This becomes all the more evident when it is borne in mind that there were concurrently many political, social and economic changes in Benin, Warri, and all along the coast between 1486 and 1841. According to Ajayi:

> The power and influence of Benin expanded and contracted; the nature of its monarchy and hence its religion were "clearly subjected to profound changes." Many people migrated to the coast to take advantage of the expanding European trade. The development of Warri as an independent state was probably part of this process. In a similar way, old fishing villages developed into the trading city-states of the Delta: Calabar, or Old Calabar as the Europeans called it; Kalabari, which they called New Calabar; Bonny and Brass; as well as Lagos and Badagri to the west.[8]

---

7. Ajayi, *Christian Missions in Nigeria*, 4. See also A. F. C. Ryder, "Missionary Activity in the Kingdom of Warri to the Early Nineteenth Century," *Journal of the Historical Society of Nigeria* 2.1, 1960.

8. Ajayi, *Christian Missions in Nigeria*, 4.

European trade dominated the lives of these states. None of them could maintain population and prosperity without it. This led to important social and political adaptations. Because of the cosmopolitan nature of the communities, the traditional social unit – the lineage or clan based on blood relationship – was replaced by the "House" in which economic and military organization counted for almost as much as kinship, and into which foreign slaves could be formally integrated. There were changes going on, but as long as the traditional rulers remained the arbiters of the destinies of their people, they saw to it that the adaptations were inspired by the traditional culture and not by the beliefs and practices of the European traders or missionaries.[9]

In fact, the unveiling of the West African coast to the modern world was a consequence of these economic interests[10] and nothing more than trade was initially contemplated:

> English commerce was soon attracted to the coast, and as this increased, a line of settlements or forts, from Gambia downwards, was planted along the seaboard, chiefly on the Slave and Gold Coasts for its protection. The benefit of the natives was not contemplated thereby. Until the beginning of this century, the commerce promoted was slave trade.[11]

According to Macgregor Laird, the legacy of commerce in the area of Calabar went back to the sixteenth century and spawned despicable moral deprivation and barbarism. Laird visited Old Calabar in 1833 out of his concern for the welfare of West Africa. In his evidence before the Parliamentary Committee in 1842, he cited Old Calabar as the most uncivilized part of Africa he had ever been to. As evidence of this, he recalled the incidence of human skulls littering the streets, a level of depravity not apparently seen in the natives of the interior.[12]

Slave trade involved the purchase and transportation of slaves by European ship owners to America to sell them to American plantation owners. Grimley and Robinson note that Europeans did not introduce slavery to Africa as it

---

9. Ajayi, *Christian Missions in Nigeria*, 4, 5. Also see K. O. Dike, *Trade and Politics in the Niger Delta* (Oxford: Oxford University Press, 1956), chs 1 and 2; D. Forde, ed., *Efik Traders of Old Calabar* (Oxford: Oxford University Press, 1957); and G. I. Jones, *Trading States of the Oil Rivers* (Oxford: Oxford University Press, 1963).

10. Goldie, *Calabar and its Mission*, 9. Goldie notes that "in 1784 that part of the continent in which Calabar lies was explored along its coastline and the name given to it by its discoverer, Diego Cam, is what is still known to Europeans."

11. Goldie, *Calabar and its Mission*, 9.

12. Goldie, *Calabar and its Mission*, 63.

already existed because of intertribal wars and war captives. The trans-Atlantic traffic in slavery merely exacerbated the practice by transforming it into a lucrative activity.[13]

However, Goldie has shown that the native serfdom of the nineteenth century was not the equivalent of the slavery that existed in the British West Indies and in the southern States of America, and that the word "slave" in this context really translates the native term that means "dependant." In his estimation, native serfdom was essentially a system of social organization that elevated might over individual rights. In this scenario, it was not uncommon for the weaker families to sell themselves to leading families for protection. Goldie has made reference to the incredible loyalty that slaves bore towards their masters:

> It is amazing how clanish the slaves belonging to the same house become. Each one considers that he partakes of the honour of the house, and is zealous in maintaining it. Any slight put upon his master, or father (the one word signifying both) as the master is designated, is resented as a personal offence.[14]

This lucrative trafficking proved to be a major factor in the shaping of the West African coast. In fact, the geography of the area in the nineteenth century was a direct result of an African "scramble" to establish strategically positioned trading posts and to cut each other out from the slave-trading ships from Europe down the river. In this "scramble," Duke Town emerged closest to the mouth of the river and thus easily became the largest and principal seat of population and traffic followed by Creek Town.[15]

---

13. Grimley and Robinson, *Church Growth in Central and Southern Nigeria*, 270.
14. Goldie, *Calabar and its Mission*, 19–20.
15. Goldie, *Calabar and its Mission*, 12, 18. It was commonly reckoned at this time that Duke Town had a population of six thousand and that Creek Town had one thousand and five hundred people. Ajayi, *Christian Missions in Nigeria*, 53, notes: "In Calabar there were three separate establishments: Creek Town, Old Town and Duke Town. There was great competition especially between Creek Town and Duke Town over the control of European trade. Further, there were internal rivalries between the various houses in each town. But in spite of these divisions, the Efik developed in the Egbo, or more correctly, Ekpe society an organization covering the whole of Calabar and superseding the sectional interest of the various Towns or the personal ambitions of the 'gentlemen,' the heads of houses of whom it was largely composed." See also H. M. Waddell, *Twenty-nine Years in the West Indies and Central Africa: a Review of Missionary Work and Adventure 1829–1858*, 2nd ed., Missionary Researches and Travels No. 11 (London: Frank Cass and Company Limited, 1870).

In the trade-driven culture of the times, it was not uncommon for chiefs to place their boys on board the ships which lay in the river awaiting their cargoes so that they might pick up a little English and knowledge of traffic:

> Any skill in reading was then gained from the notes and entries of transactions in the books of the traders, so that it was the language as written which they could read. This induced the Rev. Mr. Waddell, the pioneer of [Old Calabar] mission, to lithograph in this style the first simple lessons printed for the instruction of the natives. The name of the captains with whom the boys were placed was frequently assumed by them. Hence the name Tom Foster [for Ensa Akaha who was later to assume the title of King Eyo Honesty VII when he ascended to his uncle's throne].[16]

As Goldie notes elsewhere, this accounted for the wide-ranging knowledge of English and mathematics that the nineteenth-century missionaries encountered on the West African coast.[17] This knowledge is further evidenced by the fact that the kings and chiefs of the region, in requesting for the establishment of schools and other institutions of Western civilization from the Queen of England, did so in readable English and appended their signatures to the letters by their own hands.[18]

Grimley and Robinson credit the nineteenth-century re-introduction of Christianity to Nigeria to the notoriety of the slave trade along the West coast of Africa and the strong feeling of guilt that this generated among certain Christian groups in America and England over the cruelties against African

---

16. H. Goldie, *Memoir of King Eyo VII of Old Calabar: A Christian King in Africa* (Old Calabar: United Presbyterian Mission Press, 1894), 12. It is indicative of this trade-related heritage that King Eyo II was surnamed "Honesty" by European traders prior to the establishment of the Old Calabar Mission on account of his trustworthiness in fulfilling his engagement with them (7). "It was the custom of the principal traders to put their sons on board the vessels while they lay in the river, to acquire a smattering of English, and some of them learned to write it, while they could not write a word of their own language. Those thus taught were unaccustomed to read letterpress, but could read a page in the written form as thrown off by the lithographic press, so that the leaflets became their first books, while their contents served as texts to their instructors." Goldie, *Calabar and its Mission*, 92.

17. Goldie, *Calabar and its Mission*, 92.

18. Goldie, *Calabar and its Mission*, 73–75; Ajayi, *Christian Missions in Nigeria*, 45. Perhaps an even more revealing example is the case of King Eyo's son, whom H. M. Waddell, the leader of the first missionary party to Calabar, found already more competent in English and maths than the schoolmaster and carpenter that he brought with him. Ajayi, *Christian Missions in Nigeria*, 46.

slaves.[19] In the words of A. E. Southon, "this conscience beckoned for the extension of Christianity to these people as compensation."[20]

A fuller treatment of this sentiment and other possible causes for the Modern Missionary Movement will be explored in the following section. However, we can point out here that this sentiment belonged to a larger movement, particularly in Britain, to abolish the slave trade:

> In the early nineteenth century England led the way by passing laws against slave trade. They were joined by other countries until only Spain and Portugal continued to ply the trade, British warships were stationed along the coast where British interests were involved to intercept slave ships and free slaves. Most of these slaves were taken to Sierra Leone and put down in a strange but free land.[21]

Sierra Leone was a territory purchased in 1787 by distinguished European philanthropists along the Sierra Leone shore. They formed a settlement "for the reception of the unhappy captives rescued from the slave ships captured by British cruisers. The wretched victims of this traffic were cared for and educated."[22] Inevitably, the population of Sierra Leone was a motley collection of people from various tribes, places and speaking different languages. The territory became the prototype of Liberated African society and a model for the civilization of the African native on African soil. Mission work began early among these people by the Wesleyan and Church Missionary Societies from England.[23]

The relative success of missions and the civilizing mandate here inspired several visions aimed at transforming these Africans into agents of change to their own tribes in "heathen" Africa. The origins of the Old Calabar Mission demonstrated one such vision although, in this case, it was Jamaicans and not the Liberated Africans of Sierra Leone that were the direct agents of this "Africans to Africa" mission initiative.[24]

---

19. Grimley and Robinson, *Church Growth in Central and Southern Nigeria*, 270.
20. A. E. Southon, *Gold Coast Methodism* (London: Cargate Press, 1934), 20.
21. Grimley and Robinson, *Church Growth in Central and Southern Nigeria*, 270.
22. Goldie, *Calabar and its Mission*, 9–10. The Act of Emancipation fixed 1 August 1834 as the day in which the new era should begin for the serfs of West Indian islands (67).
23. Grimley and Robinson, *Church Growth in Central and Southern Nigeria*, 270.
24. Ajayi, *Christian Missions to Nigeria*, 43–44; J. McKerrow, *History of the Foreign Missions of the Secession and United Presbyterian Church* (Edinburgh, 1867), 368–69; Goldie, *Calabar and its Mission*, 73; and Dickie, *Story of the Mission in Old Calabar*, 11.

The commitment to civilize Africa as an inseparable counterpart to mission underscores a very important element of the Modern Missionary Movement to Africa. Christian conscience, which Grimley and Robinson consider to be the cause of this movement, did not undermine the nearly unanimous perception in Europe that the tribes of the Dark Continent belonged to an inferior race and culture(s). Rather, it necessitated a different approach to mission in Africa than was admissible elsewhere:

> The Asiatic nations are advanced in civilization; while the Negro tribes of Africa are in a condition of utter barbarism. The former are in possession of languages and literature which were cultivated when Britain lay in darkness; the latter are quite unlettered. It is manifest that the mode of mission work must in many respects be different to suit these two extremes.[25]

Goldie makes the point that whereas cross-cultural mission fundamentally entails an attitude of kindness, gentleness and humility, in order for the missionary to enter into the lives of a strange people and to secure the leverage necessary to impact them for change, the challenges posed by different mission fields affect methodology:

> In the cultured nations of Asia, the assurance of their own superiority to the teacher will produce the feeling that they need not the instruction of his wisdom. Among the African tribes we find our difficulty in reaching them is of a different kind. They are men; we are more than men; consequently they have nothing in common with us. The truth we endeavour to convey to them belongs to us to believe and practise.[26]

The biblical account of the evangelization of Philippi, a Roman colony in the days of the Roman Empire (Acts 16:11–40), and of Paul's entire mission to the Gentiles who generally enjoyed a higher socio-political status than the Palestinian Jew of the time, presents a very striking parallel in terms of what the status of the missionary, when compared to that of the peoples of the mission field, does to methodology. The magistrates of Philippi could limit the freedoms of the missionaries in response to the accusations of some of their citizens and administered corporal punishment to the latter without giving the

---

25. Goldie, *Calabar and its Mission*, 322.
26. Goldie, *Calabar and its Mission*, 322–23.

accused the opportunity to defend themselves. It was mission "from under," not mission "from above" the unconverted.

In nineteenth-century Africa, when it came to dealing with the "inferior" African, the onus for the recognition of the African's contributions and epistemological assets lay squarely on the shoulders of the European missionary. The missionary had to find within himself and his faith the rationale to accept and honour common brotherhood with the clearly disadvantaged native. In Goldie's estimation, this was only possible in those who were under what he called the Christian principle. Those who lacked it and found themselves among inferior races saw themselves as the standard by which all others are judged. Consequently, they looked down on Africans with contempt, and when they had Africans in their power, denied them the equal rights of humanity.[27]

Goldie uses the term "inferior" without qualification. However, his sentiments below suggest that he, as David Livingstone did, attributed this inferiority to merely circumstantial reasons and not ontological ones.

The perceived superiority of the Europeans is evidenced by the overwhelming sense of paternalism that accompanied Modern Missions to Africa in general and Old Calabar in particular. As late as 1894, Goldie writes that "the tribes of the dark continent" were considered

> By superior races as made to be enslaved or destroyed . . . The European powers which have divided the territory of the dark-skinned tribes amongst themselves, by entering into engagements to protect them so far from these of destruction, have given a hope that they will use their power to promote the gracious purpose of our common Father, that the Negro shall have his equal place among his fellow-men. But the hope is yet distant of accomplishment.[28]

It is also evidenced by the fact that the few whose opinions were the exception to the rule, people like David Livingstone and Henry Venn, were so influenced by Scriptural teaching that they were able to defy popular opinion.

We have already encountered Ajayi's claim that the failure of Christian missions to West Africa between the fifteenth and seventeenth centuries lay in a failure by missionaries to engage the world view of the African.[29] In his estimation, the evangelical Christianity of the nineteenth and twentieth

---

27. Goldie, *Calabar and its Mission*, 323.
28. Goldie, *Memoir of King Eyo VII*, 3.
29. Ajayi, *Christian Missions to Nigeria*, 4.

centuries was even more scandalized by African ritual, dancing and finery in religious ceremonies and distrusted them in social life. It was also decidedly more individualistic and insensitive to the holism of the African world view. Its two redeeming features were a strong and indomitable faith, and "a certain egalitarian belief that while all men were sinners until 'regenerated,' all were equally capable of 'regeneration.'"[30]

However, in the heat of an emboldened European hegemony following the colonization of most of Africa at the end of the nineteenth century, it was not uncommon to hear comments that suggested that the African soul was harder to transform, even by the grace of God, than the white soul. This slide in the esteem of African abilities at times included scepticism about the African's ability to be civilized.

The "African character" was becoming for many Europeans synonymous with lying, hypocrisy, drunkenness and immorality. Bishop Crowther, formerly a Liberated African slave from Sierra Leone, and his men were soon being caricatured as spoilt Africans, masquerading in borrowed tweeds, learned perhaps, but without the heritage that even the most profane, untutored, perverse European could claim of centuries of Christian culture and civilization. The African was on his way to becoming "half devil, half child."[31] This attitude, though it appeared so suddenly in the missions in Nigeria, had a more gradual growth in England and was in part the making of the publications of the earlier missionaries, both Europeans and Africans.[32]

There is ample evidence that the European of the nineteenth century understood himself or herself to be a member of a higher society and system of life than the African. This is ably demonstrated by the scarcity or conspicuous standing of Europeans who saw the African as at least of equal potential with the European and deserving of all the opportunities that would enable his or her ascent from backwardness. Among them was Dr. David Livingstone (1813–1873). He differed from most of his contemporaries in his estimation of the African by attributing all the differences within humanity to, mostly, external circumstances. In his understanding of the teaching of the Bible, he

---

30. Ajayi, *Christian Missions to Nigeria*, 8.

31. This phrase is from Kipling's poem "The White Man's Burden" (for the full text see: https://www.kiplingsociety.co.uk/poem/poems_burden.htm).

32. Walls, "Samuel Ajayi Crowther 1807–1891," 261, 264.

found the incontrovertible proof of the equality of all the races to lie in their "inward unity of thought, passion, prejudice, sympathy, [and] desire."[33]

Another was Henry Venn, Honorary Secretary of the Parent Committee of the Church Missionary Society from 1841 to 1872. He is noted for urging the training and employment of Africans more as a virtue than as a measure of the economy meant to cut down on expenditure by retaining Africans in the colonies as they cost less to maintain than Europeans. His legacy to missions lies in his conviction that "the missionary who did not prepare for the day when he would no longer be in the mission by raising up an indigenous clergy and episcopacy was building on sand."[34]

However, the perceived superiority of the European was not exclusively held by Europeans but also shared by a vast majority of Africans. This reality can be seen in the proliferation of Western lifestyles and the acquisition of numerous artefacts of Western civilization by those Africans who had the means to do so.

Ajayi has argued that this was, for a while, a very selective appropriation of Western civilization by the Africans. After acknowledging the wanton excess of the material artefacts of Western civilization in the houses of the leading members of Old Calabar,[35] he points out that there was a deliberate movement by Africans to limit this cultural influence:

> Not one of the coastal states, so much in touch with Europeans for so long adopted the religion or the system of government, taxation, or justice of their European customers and teachers. Rather, while continuing to trade, the coastal peoples deliberately erected barriers to shut off European cultural influence . . . [Apart from the houses built by missionaries in Benin and Warri and the barracoons and tenements built by Portuguese and Brazilian traders on the beach, some distance from the town of Lagos], it became a firm policy throughout the coast to prevent Europeans

---

33. *Dr. Livingstone's Cambridge Lectures: together with a prefatory letter by the Rev. Professor Sedgewick* (Cambridge: Deighton, Bell, 1858), 83, 84; Ajayi, *Christian Missions in Nigeria*, 173, 175.

34. In the words of Ajayi, "Venn's greatest claim to the commanding position he came to occupy in the history of the expansion of the church was the way in which he developed these ideas into something like a Code of missions" (*Christian Missions to Nigeria*, 175). See also W. Knight, *The Missionary Secretariat of Henry Venn* (London, 1882), 417; J. N. K. Mugambi, *From Liberation to Reconstruction: African Christian Theology After the Cold War* (Nairobi, Kenya: East African Educational Publishers Ltd., 1995), 91; and S. C. Neil, *A History of Christian Missions* (Harmondsworth: Penguin, 1964), 259–60.

35. Ajayi, *Christian Missions in Nigeria*, 6.

from building on land to confine them to their trading hulks. Apart from restrictive laws, the coastal states erected cultural barriers. They tended to formalise the organization and training of the traditional cults as an answer to the formal organization and training of the European missionaries. Further, they developed new integrative societies like the Ekpe of Calabar, and exploited to the full the traditional cults and religious festivals as symbols of cultural identity.[36]

However, with the advent of nineteenth-century missions and the more or less permanent resident status of its missionaries both along the coastal areas and, eventually, inland, these inhibitions were breached. The forces of civilization resumed their march to conquer Africa supported by an ever-increasing European involvement in Africa. Civilization was essentially viewed as attaining to and acquiring what was viewed as best in European life.

Ajayi notes that

> Buxton and the missionaries who shared his view meant by civilization more than was implicit in membership of the Church. Civilization meant to them all what they considered best in their own way of life. In the first place, they expected conformity to their own social manners and customs. They insisted on even minor observances as necessary outward and visible signs of an inward "civilized" state. There was a proper and improper way of doing things in Victorian England. And many of the customs and habits were regarded not just as unimportant matters of social convenience; to the missionary, each had a religious significance.[37]

As an example, he cites the English custom of bowing as contrasted with the African custom of prostrating oneself before one's elders as a sign of respect. The latter was viewed as implying a sinful element of worshipping a human being. In the same vein, Dickie recounts how in 1848, the people of Old Calabar, whose "marriage customs are singularly absurd, as well as painfully degrading," received their "first and much-needed object lesson in marriage." This occasion was the marriage of Henry Hamilton and Mary Brown, two of the Blacks who came from Jamaica with the missionary band. Hamilton

---

36. Ajayi, *Christian Missions in Nigeria*, 7. See also G. Parrinder, *West African Religion* (London, 1949).

37. Ajayi, *Christian Missions in Nigeria*, 14.

did not have to pay dowry for his bride – apparently one of the absurdities undermined by this "Christian" wedding.[38]

The above is the world in which the Old Calabar Mission was hatched and nurtured. In the ensuing section, we will focus on this mission in order to provide the most immediate context of the translation of the Efik New Testament.

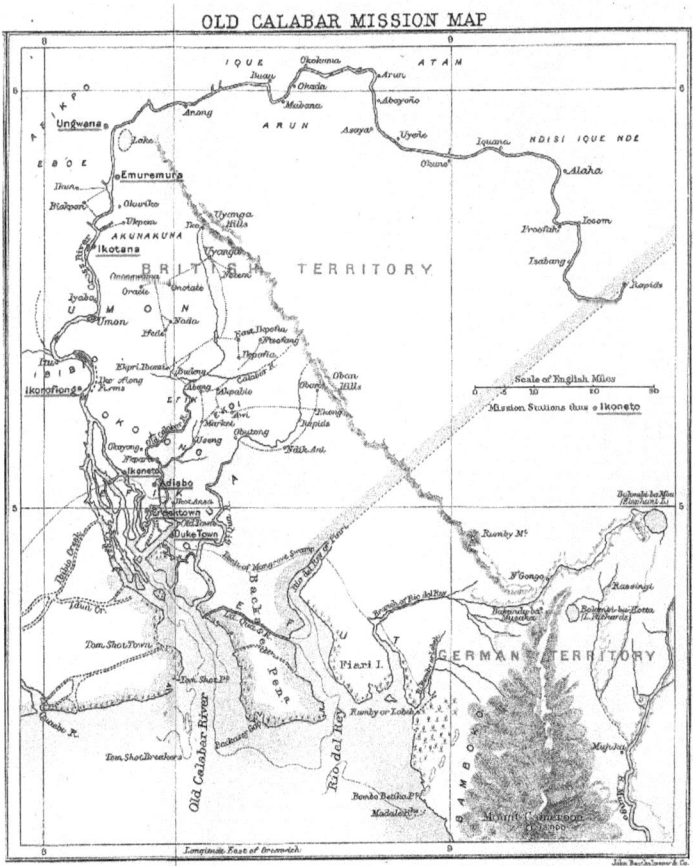

Figure 1. Map of Old Calabar.[39]

---

38. Dickie, *Story of the Mission in Old Calabar*, 33–35.
39. Dickie, *Story of the Mission in Old Calabar*, 101.

4

Origins and History: Old Calabar Mission

The Modern Missionary Movement was a consequence of, largely,
The evangelical revival of the late eighteenth-century that owed so much to the work of John Wesley. This revival created a new and growing Methodist Church and an increasingly powerful evangelical party within the established Anglican Church. It infected all Protestants in Europe and North America with a new fervour and zeal in religious matters which resulted in the foundations of various missionary societies in the last decade of the century.[1]

We have already noted the two redeeming features of evangelical Christianity, according to Ajayi: a strong and indomitable faith, and the belief that all sinners were equally capable of regeneration. It was not long before these convictions led evangelical leaders like Wesley

> beyond the Enlightenment-inspired ideas of "the noble savage" for the native, into an understanding that this savage was a sinner and degenerate idolater in need of regeneration. Slavery was not just a cruel and inhuman practice that should be improved but a sin that must be abolished. In this way Wesley brought the whole weight of the evangelical revival behind the anti-slavery movement.[2]

By and large, the Niger Expedition of 1841 was a product of evangelical pressure on the British Government to tackle slave trade at its source by

---

1. Ajayi, *Christian Missions in Nigeria*, 7–8.
2. Ajayi, *Christian Missions in Nigeria*, 9.

transforming the world view, lifestyles and social systems of the Africans. In the words of Buxton, an evangelical leader of the anti-slavery movement,

> We must elevate the minds of her [Africa's] people and call for the resources of her soil . . . Let missionaries and schoolmasters, the plough and the spade, go together and agriculture; the avenues to legitimate commerce will be opened; confidence between man and man will be inspired; whilst civilization will advance as the natural effect, and Christianity operate as the proximate cause, of this happy change.[3]

To execute this plan, Buxton urged the British government to undertake pioneer expeditions through the large waterways into the interior in order to make treaties with chiefs and to demonstrate what opportunities there were for private capital; that industrialists and merchants should follow the lead of the government and invest capital in the development of Africa.[4]

This perception was, by no means, without opposition:

> Slave-owning and extreme evangelicals continued to protest against it on the grounds that slavery was a social and economic, not spiritual matter and it was obscuring the line of division between temporal and spiritual matters. But the main body of evangelicals saw in the anti-slavery campaign a challenge with which to awaken the conscience of the Christian to do his duty to his neighbour.[5]

In this, Buxton and the anti-slavery movement were facilitating, for West Africa, the vision that David Livingstone had for Central Africa.[6] It is quite clear, then, that, from the very onset, the Modern Missionary Movement was intent on using cultural, economic and military superiority[7] to implement its

---

3. T. F. Buxton, *The African Slave Trade and its Remedy* (London, 1840), 282, 511; Ajayi, *Christian Missions in Nigeria*, 10–12.

4. Ajayi, *Christian Missions in Nigeria*, 11. See allso W. Allen and T. R. H. Thomas, *Narrative of the Expedition to the River Niger in 1841*, 2 vols. (London, 1848); J. F. Schon and S. Crowther, *Journals of the Expedition of 1841* (CMS, 1842).

5. Ajayi, *Christian Missions in Nigeria*, 9. See also "Thoughts on Slavery" in *The Complete Works of John Wesley*, vol. XI (London, 1872), 64–65.

6. Ross, *Blantyre Mission*, 14–16. We have already noted Livingstone's views and suggestions about the barriers preventing the new life that the gospel brings from coming to fruition in Africa.

7. Europe's economic and military superiority were self-evident as the "scramble" by West Africans for a piece of European civilization demonstrates. However, cultural superiority was not as easily recognized by the Africans as the account above also demonstrates.

agenda for Africa. This agenda was generally aimed at no less than a complete overhaul of African societies.

In keeping with their functional and alleged ontological superiority, the Europeans' approach to the task presupposed downgrading African social and political systems. Ajayi notes that in the expansion of the Christian missions in the period 1853–60 there was a total indifference to the political institutions of the people:

> The missionaries began in Badagri and Calabar by trying to strengthen the hands of the traditional rulers and using their power to protect and further the cause of the missions. But the availability of the naval power of Britain was too tempting an alternative; they began to shield behind the navy and in consequence helped to weaken the political power of the states.[8]

It also entailed trivializing the rationality and capabilities of Africans.[9]

The Niger Expedition was a huge disaster. However, this did not kill the momentum and popularity of Buxton's ideas:

> In 1843, the African Civilization Society and the Agricultural Society were disbanded. Buxton died broken-hearted two years later. Nevertheless, his influence did not die with him. Between 1839 and 1842 he had given the Niger as much publicity in Europe as any other African territory not the scene of war or within the path of the charismatic David Livingstone . . . [However], Buxton had achieved a far-reaching change in government policy. Hitherto generally averse to getting involved in West African local politics, the government now began to encourage the signing of slave-trade treaties to strengthen the hands of its naval officers by securing for them the support of favourably disposed African rulers on the mainland. That meant that the missionaries could now bank on more effective protection from the anti-slavery preventive squadron.[10]

In retrospect, therefore, the Niger Expedition marks the beginning of the new missionary enterprise in Nigeria. "The publicity set in motion

---

8. Ajayi, *Christian Missions in Nigeria*, 99.

9. See Goldie's evaluation of how the position of a people on the universal scale of valuation directly impacts mission method. *Calabar and its Mission*, 322–23.

10. Ajayi, *Christian Missions in Nigeria*, 13.

a train of events which the failure of the expedition could not hold back."[11] In particular, the wide publicity ignited and consolidated the intentions of liberated slaves in Sierra Leone and elsewhere to return to their homelands. For mission organizations, these intentions presented an opportunity to use newly emancipated free men as agents to carry the gospel "which had done so much for them, to their degraded kindred in Africa."[12]

In Goshen, Jamaica, the arrival of a copy of Buxton's *The African Slave Trade and its Remedy* was to prove to be the decisive spark. One of Buxton's arguments was that the providence of God had overruled slavery and the slave trade so that from

> the settlers of Sierra Leone, the peasantry of the West Indies, and the thousands of their children now receiving a Christian education, may be expected to arise a body of men, who will return to the land of their fathers, carrying divine truth and all its concomitant blessings to the heart of Africa.[13]

According to an account of the occasion, "this book was greedily perused; and so much light did it cast upon the problem, that an express messenger was sent to Kingston to buy up a dozen copies which had just reached there, so that each congregation had a copy."[14]

The particular session of the Jamaica Presbytery at Goshen, St. Mary's parish,[15] 1841, that took the decisive step to establish a mission in Calabar, was extraordinary for its singleness of purpose and commitment:

> We felt bound to take some decided step, yet seeing that the general consequences would result to ourselves and our congregations from our decision, we suspended business, and under inexpressible solemnity of mind, devoted the rest of the day to prayer for Divine direction. When the subject was resumed next morning, a deep feeling of awe was on the minds of all present, as each gave his

---

11. Ajayi, *Christian Missions in Nigeria*, 13. See also J. Gallagher, "Fowell Buxton and the New African Policy," in *Cambridge Historical Journal* XI, 1950.

12. Ajayi, *Christian Missions in Nigeria*, 13. Apparently, even leaving Sierra Leone for the hinterland of Africa was perceived as leaving a place where God was known for a land of darkness (29). Also see Goldie, *Calabar and its Mission*, 69.

13. Dickie, *Story of the Mission in Old Calabar*, 10.

14. Dickie, *Story of the Mission in Old Calabar*, 9.

15. The Jamaica Presbytery was composed of agents of the Scottish Missionary Society, most of them ministers of the United Secession Church. Dickie, *Story of the Mission in Old Calabar*, 11.

opinion in favour of the new mission, and expressed his readiness to go forth on it, if called by his brethren, and approved by the church at home. It was a renewed, unreserved self-consecration to the cause of our Lord and Saviour among the heathen.[16]

As one of the resolutions passed and presented to their churches for adoption indicates, there was no doubt in the members' minds that they were committing themselves to a particularly depraved people, compelled by divine will and a sure word of prophecy:

> That the long-neglected and critical condition of the inhabitants of that vast country, hitherto sunk in the deepest darkness, and exposed to all the miseries of the most iniquitous system that ever defiled or desolated the earth, together with the duty which the Church owes to the Lord Jesus to go into all the world and preach the Gospel to every creature, and the Divine prediction apparently about to be fulfilled – Ethiopia shall soon stretch out her hand to God, – demand of us most seriously to consider our duty in that solemn and important matter.[17]

Not surprisingly, the boldness of the enterprise alarmed their friends in Scotland. That the little Jamaica Presbytery, themselves dependent on the churches at home, would adopt such a venture was viewed as presumption. Moreover, the recent failure of the better-organized and funded Niger Expedition and the fact that other missionary enterprises in Africa were incurring heavy losses[18] seemed to underscore the folly of embarking on such an enterprise.[19]

However, in Dickie's aggrandizing terms, "others [who] had that 'divine insanity of noble minds,' which counts truth more precious than life, and the cause and command of Christ more to be respected than death," prevailed.[20] No doubt, this "nobility" of mind was not a little aided by the fact that the

---

16. Waddell, *Twenty-Nine Years in the West Indies and Central Africa*, 206.

17. McKerrow, *History of the Foreign Missions*, 369. See also Goldie, *Calabar and its Mission*, 71, 72. In the words of Dickie, "the scene had a moral sublimity of its own – the grandeur of the object; the apparent impotence of the means; the conviction that 'all power' would be with them. 'Do you ask how I felt?' says Miss Jameson, who was present; 'I was lifted above myself at the noble bravery of the men.'" *Story of the Mission in Old Calabar*, 10–11.

18. Thirty-one out of eighty-nine had, within twelve months of their arrival, fallen in Sierra Leone; seven out of twelve in Liberia; whilst two bands of nine men shortly after setting foot on the Gold Coast, had been exterminated by fever. Dickie, *Story of the Mission in Old Calabar*, 11.

19. Goldie, *Calabar and its Mission*, 72–73; Dickie, *Story of the Mission in Old Calabar*, 11.

20. Dickie, *Story of the Mission in Old Calabar*, 11.

Jamaica Presbytery, upon receiving positive news from their emissary to the rulers of Calabar,[21] were willing to proceed with the mission with or without the approval of the Scottish Missionary Society in Scotland.[22] Towards this end,

> The missionaries met at Hampden, September 1843, and agreed to form a society to carry out their design, and elected the Rev. H. M. Waddell as leader thereof. While thus making arrangements in Jamaica, the synod of the United Presbyterian Church held its annual meeting in Glasgow, 1844, and unanimously resolved to adopt the mission to Calabar, and instructed the committee then superintending the foreign missions of the denomination to co-operate with the Jamaica Presbytery in carrying it out.[23]

As it happened, the interest of the Jamaica Presbytery in Calabar was matched by requests from both King Eyamba of Duke Town and King Eyo of Creek Town for assistance, through European messengers, from the Queen of England. They wanted to set up an agricultural base in Calabar for trade, now that they had signed a treaty for abandoning the slave trade.[24]

It is quite clear from this that the rulers of Calabar were interested in cooperating with the agents of European missionary organizations fundamentally for trade-related reasons.[25] With the demise of the slave trade, palm oil had become the chief commodity of an ongoing relationship with Europeans:

> To them, the British campaign was only another phase of the struggle that had been going on for generations between various

---

21. A certain Captain Turner, captain of one of the ships conducting trade in Calabar brought the official letter of offer from King Eyamba the Fifth and Seven Chiefs in response to the proposals of Messrs. George Blyth and Peter Anderson, missionaries of the Jamaica Presbytery on furlough in Scotland in 1842. The two missionaries used their furlough to canvass for the idea of a West African mission in various churches and to engage the rulers of Calabar in discussions. Goldie, *Calabar and its Mission*, 74–75.

22. The initial reply from the Scottish Missionary Society that prompted the above reaction from Jamaica was very blunt. It labelled the proposal as "premature, displaying more zeal than judgement, not accordant with the state of dependence in which our Jamaica Church stood, both for means and missionaries; highly presumptuous after the failure of vastly greater efforts by others than we could possibly put forth." D. M. McFarlan, *Calabar, the Church of Scotland Mission, 1846–1946* (Edinburgh, 1946), 7; Goldie, *Calabar and its Mission*, 72–73.

23. Goldie, *Calabar and its Mission*, 75–76.

24. Ajayi, *Christian Missions in Nigeria*, 73–74.

25. Apparently, Waddell ended up supporting this orientation upon discovering, when he landed in Calabar in 1846, that "particularly in the Delta, trade, not agriculture was the civilizing force, and that the chiefs were not a 'land-owning aristocracy' but middle-class traders." Ajayi, *Christian Missions in Nigeria*, 46, 55–56.

European nations competing for the lion's share of the trade on the coast. The English had changed their article of trade; for reasons not quite clear to the Delta people, they began to refuse to deal in slaves, and were calling, more and more for palm-oil, for elephant's tooth, camwood and gum opal. Their intention to capture the market remained the same, however; they brought warships to fight their Portuguese and Spanish, Brazilian and French rivals.[26]

In his biographical publication of King Eyo Honesty VII, Goldie notes that the rule of life of the earlier King Eyo Honesty II was the maxim given him by Duke Efium: "keep to your trade, and your trade will keep you." This accounts for the overwhelmingly open welcome and cooperation that Waddell and his team received when they landed in 1846 in the Delta region.[27]

In fact, the rulers of the Delta were shown to be keener than Africans in other coastal areas to acquire the input of Europeans. In their desire to see agricultural development and education come to them, "they declared themselves willing to pay for services received. Like shrewd businessmen, they haggled over the terms on which the missionaries were allowed to settle."[28] According to Commander Raymond, who brokered the anti-slavery treaty in 1842, nowhere else on the coast were the people so anxious to be civilized.[29]

However, the interests of the people of Calabar were broader than mere trade, in keeping with the nature of the promises made by the British government.[30] They were looking for a new era of prosperity and were willing

---

26. Ajayi, *Christian Missions in Nigeria*, 54; Goldie, *Memoir of King Eyo VII*, 8.

27. Waddell and his team were personally welcomed by King Eyo of Creek Town and, soon after, King Eyamba of Duke Town. With the utmost expediency, one of the prime pieces of property in Duke Town was allocated to the mission. Dickie, *Story of the Mission in Old Calabar*, 14–16. But perhaps the best indicator of this openness is how King Eyo offered his courtyard as a missionary centre and personally interpreted for Mr. Waddell until an alternative interpreter was trained (19). See also Goldie, *Memoir of King Eyo VII*, 10–11.

28. Ajayi, *Christian Missions in Nigeria*, 56. Further, whereas the chiefs of Bonny agreed to lease land for mission settlement for only a period of twenty years, the rulers of Calabar guaranteed the lease of the land used by missionaries indefinitely and even offered free labour for the task of building it. McFarlan, *Calabar, the Church of Scotland Mission*, 7; Ajayi, *Christian Missions in Nigeria*, 112.

29. Commander Raymond to Foote, 11 Dec. 1842, cited in Ajayi, *Christian Missions in Nigeria*, 100.

30. The new proposals that England began to make in 1839 were examined very critically. It appeared that England was offering not only hopes of increased trade, but also hopes of a more equitable, less one-sided trade than the merchants of the coast had hitherto engaged in. These included canals, manufacture of paper, and use of printing presses; affording essential assistance to the natives by furnishing them with useful information as to the best mode of cultivation, and productions which are marketable; introducing improved agricultural implements and

to pay the price of having their cultural impregnability breached by allowing the missionaries to build and live in their midst. Yet even in this, they attempted to draw the line at stopping missionaries from owning mission land.[31]

Given the superior status that the missionaries enjoyed among Africans, it was not long before they began to assume the role of master and judge. Missionaries and traders teamed up; with the support of the naval squadron not far away and the Governor of the Spanish island of Fernando Po, who happened to be an Englishman,[32] they began to agitate for radical changes according to their estimation of what was acceptable and not acceptable.

Waddell immediately stopped the practice of casting corpses of slaves, who were not esteemed as equal human beings,[33] into the bushes of the land allocated to the mission.[34] When the king's brother, John Duke, died and about one hundred slaves were killed to satisfy the dignity of the deceased as his retinue in the afterlife, Waddell rounded up the chiefs responsible for the execution of the custom and "put the fear of divine retribution in their hearts."[35]

Back in Britain, Waddell's submissions before the Hutt Committee[36] included a plea that, in addition to efforts to prevent the selling of slaves on the coast, it must "use all its influence with the native authorities to prevent their killing slaves, for it is certainly just as bad to kill them as to sell them, and perhaps worse."[37]

---

seeds; and the possibility of introducing the steam engine. "Prospectus of the Society for the Extinction of the Slave Trade and the Civilisation of Africa," instituted June 1839, in Buxton, *The African Slave Trade and its Remedy*, 8–16. For the extent to which this prospectus informed official British aspirations in Africa during the era of full-blown colonialism, see Johnston, *The Backward Peoples and Our Relations with Them*, 7, 42, 56, 59.

31. Ajayi, *Christian Missions in Nigeria*, 56.

32. In the absence of an official British official, John Beecroft, the Governor of Fernando Po, filled the role of British Consul. In May 1849, he was formally appointed Her Majesty's Consul in the Bights of Benin and Biafra and supervised the Niger Delta from Fernando Po. Ajayi, *Christian Missions in Nigeria*, 60, 61.

33. In this highly hierarchical society, slaves were at the bottom of the ladder. It was appropriate, for example, to execute one's slaves as a sign of sorrowing for a loved one who had died. It is hardly surprising, therefore, that they were deemed unworthy of burial when they died and were merely tossed in the bush to rot. Dickie, *Story of the Mission in Old Calabar*, 21.

34. Dickie, *Story of the Mission in Old Calabar*, 16, 21.

35. Dickie, *Story of the Mission in Old Calabar*, 22.

36. William Hutt, M.P. was the Chairman of a Select Committee of the House of Commons that recommended a withdrawal of the naval squadron from West Africa in 1849. The government overturned this recommendation. Ajayi, *Christian Missions in Nigeria*, 61.

37. Ajayi, *Christian Missions in Nigeria*, 64.

> Waddell proposed that the naval squadron should go further than the matter of the external slave trade and undertake the abolition of human sacrifice, a matter of internal reform. Even before the British government accepted the argument and included this clause in the new treaty forms, the missionaries in Calabar had taken steps to see such a measure enforced.[38]

In the wake of the deaths of two notables in Duke Town and rumours of human sacrifice at their funerals, the Europeans pressured the Ekpe societies of Duke Town and Creek Town to pass a law abolishing the practice. Further, they formed a society intended to abolish superstitions and customs deemed inhuman by the society and to promote civilization.

William Anderson, the missionary in charge of Duke Town, "feeling that a united moral force on the part of all white people in the neighbourhood whether missionary or trader was fully warranted if not imperatively called for," convened a meeting at the mission house. Ten supercargoes, one of them a Dutchman, three surgeons, Edgerly (the missionary in Old Town), and Anderson himself met and "resolved that all present go in a body to King Archibong and the gentlemen of Duke Town at 5 p.m. and denounce the murders committed on Tuesday and to protest the recurrence of such barbarities." The protest meeting was duly held and King Archibong and the gentry said they would like to meet the rulers of Creek Town and take common action. The following day the reformers met and resolved to form themselves into a "permanent Society for the suppression of human sacrifices in Old Calabar or the destruction of human life in any way, except as the penalty of crime."[39]

> They met King Eyo of Creek Town and threatened to break off all intercourse unless an Ekepe law was passed within a month to that effect. On Friday, 15 February such a law was solemnly proclaimed in both Duke Town and Creek Town. The new society then met to discuss how such a law extended to the neighbouring towns and ensure its strict observance. By then Hope Waddell had arrived and it was he who proposed the motion, which was carried unanimously, that the aims of the society be broadened, and the name be changed to the Society for the Abolition of Inhuman and

---

38. Ajayi, *Christian Missions in Nigeria*, 64.
39. Ajayi, *Christian Missions in Nigeria*, 64.

Superstitious Customs and for promoting Civilization in Calabar (hereinafter referred to as SAISC).[40]

Perhaps the most graphic indicator of the rise of European hegemony and the loss of the natives' power to determine their own lives was the blowing up of Old Town in 1854 by a British gunboat. The reason was for perpetuating the ordeal[41] in order to ascertain the "cause" of the death of its chief, Willy Tom, contrary to a recently passed law. This was done at the initial instigation of Mrs. Edgerley and Mr. Thomson, resident missionaries at the place. After blowing up the town, the officers of the British gunboat forbade its rebuilding.

However, Ajayi observes that, after pointing out the eagerness with which Edgerley reported that there was human sacrifice at the chief's funeral and with which he demanded and pursued punishment for the culprits, thereby providing the initial pretext for the destruction of Old Town, the missionaries opposed the bombardment and burning of the town. They did so to stem native resentment because they saw native instrumentality and cooperation as indispensable to native moral reformation. In the end, the deed was the contrivance of the traders and the supercargoes, who thought a show of British force would help them in their dealings with Duke Town and Creek Town.[42]

Following this, the fate of the natives of Calabar was now in the hands of the coalition of traders, missionaries and the British presence in the Consul and the navy squadron. Whatever good came out of this scenario was at the discretion of this coalition. Ajayi recounts how the Mission House, technically under the civil authority of local rulers, housed missionaries who regarded themselves as above this jurisdiction. "Waddell thought that he solved the situation by saying that the local civil authority, however crude, must be regarded as rulers of their people, Christian or unconverted, 'though we should not regard them as our rulers.'"[43]

---

40. Ajayi, *Christian Missions in Nigeria*, 64–65. See also Waddell, entry for 19 Feb. 1850, *Journals*, vol. VII, 94.

41. The ordeal was the practice of determining causes using black magic.

42. Dickie, *Story of the Mission in Old Calabar*, 47–48. Ajayi, *Christian Missions in Nigeria*, 119.

43. Ajayi, *Christian Missions in Nigeria*, 117. See also Waddell, entry for Tuesday 4 Dec. 1849, *Journals*, vol. VII, 95. In doing this, the missionaries understood themselves as having established in the Mission House, the equivalent of "a city of refuge" for the innocent "in this land of blood." Anderson's journal entry for 31 May 1849, in U.P. *Missionary Record*, 1850, 25, cited in Ajayi, *Christian Missions in Nigeria*, 118. "How far each Mission House was a 'city of refuge' depended to some extent on the theology of each missionary, but to a greater extent on the ability of the local rulers to resist European visitors tempted to take the law into their own hands" (118).

In Ajayi's estimation, this change of tactics was a consequence of the frustration and impatience by the missionaries at the sluggish pace at which change was happening:

> When Waddell and the missionaries could no longer control their impatience they turned to the "moral" force of the traders and the physical force of the consul and the naval squadron to achieve reform through the Society for the abolition of Inhuman and Superstitious Customs in Calabar.[44]

In this shift in the balance of power, persuasion was substituted with coercion.[45]

It would be inaccurate to leave the impression that all this reform, in spite of the attitudes and methods, was idealistically opposed by every African and, in all instances, forced upon the Calabarese. King Eyo Honesty II, for one, agreed in essence that many of the customs of his tribe were barbarous and in need of change. He also understood the advantages of the white man's knowledge and took it upon himself to cooperate with the missionaries in any way possible.

We have already noted his exemplary cooperation in Old Calabar, to the point of assuming the role of interpreter for the missionaries. Even the otherwise unimpressionable Dickie adopts an appreciative tone when writing about him. To Dickie, King Eyamba's palace was an inappropriately furnished contraption imported from Liverpool (14); the heathenism of the Calabarese was quite inhuman (16) and pathetic (18); King Eyamba's eating habits were, at best, "strange" (16); the gentility were a ridiculous affront to the concept of "gentleman" (16–17); their funeral rites were "ghastly" and "barbarous" and "a strange commentary on the savage mind" (22–23); several others of their customs revealed traces of totenism (24–25). The natives were characteristically savage (28); their marriage customs "singularly absurd, as well as painfully degrading" (33); and the pioneers' work was "to drive out of the land the rank superstitions and horrible customs under which the people were held down as under a heel of iron" (32).

Yet, in writing of King Eyo Honesty II, he lauds him as "a sagacious, clever, honest, open-faced man" dressed in "native grandeur" and who presented himself as "one of nature's gentlemen – courteous, sober-living, and just" (14);

---

44. Ajayi, *Christian Missions in Nigeria*, 102.

45. "There were a number of other missionaries who confused rudeness to people, rulers and goals alike, with courageous zeal . . . Edgerley, at Old Town, Calabar, was like Mann in his ill-controlled temper and superior attitudes. In 1849 in a fit of temper following a minor conflict, he broke the Ekpe drum at the local Town Hall." Ajayi, *Christian Missions in Nigeria*, 118–19.

an enlightened man . . . anxious to see the abolition of many of the heathen and cruel customs of his people, but . . . too prudent to compel obedience" (19); one in whose town missionary work progressed quickly (19). Of his legacy he notes that "although he never identified himself with the cause which he did much to favour, yet by his tact, prudence, common sense, and charitableness he allowed Christianity to make itself a place in Creek Town which it has never lost" (62–63). And, upon his death, "there was not a drop of blood shed" (63).[46]

Yet even King Eyo Honesty II was "rather chagrined that the white people should be urging upon him in matters of internal government." In addition, he was not convinced that change should all happen at once without giving customs and prejudices time to evolve.[47] In Ajayi's words, "the Efik King regarded religion as an affair of the community, whose customs and practices could only be changed when the community became generally convinced of the need for change."[48]

Consequently, he wanted to moderate the pace of change and actively opposed some missionary-initiated reforms aimed at legislating spiritual transformation.[49] One such initiative was the idea of making school-attending boys to sign papers committing themselves to further reform. Another was the resolution to ask every slave owner to sign a declaration on being admitted into the fellowship of the church that bound him to observing all the reforms that the missionaries had worked out. The wording of this declaration is indicative of the extent to which matters of spiritual judgement were being made into law:

> Believing that all men are equal in the sight of God, and that, under the gospel, there is in Christ neither bond nor free, I hereby, as a servant of Christ, bound to obey the commands of God's word, promise, in the sight of the great God, my divine Master, that I shall regard those persons placed under my care, and formerly held by me as slaves, as *servants*, and not *property*; that I shall encourage them to obtain education for themselves and their children, and to attend on such means of religious instruction as the Church may be able to afford them; that I shall dispose of none of them for the mere purposes of gain; that I shall do so only in the case of those who, being chargeable with criminal offences, would be liable to be put to death were they to remain in Calabar,

---

46. Dickie, *Memoir of King Eyo VII*, 10.
47. Waddell, entry for 3 Oct. 1850, *Journals*, vol. VIII, 72.
48. Ajayi, *Christian Missions in Nigeria*, 102.
49. Ajayi, *Christian Missions in Nigeria*, 102.

and who can be legally banished in no other way; and that I shall endeavour as far as I can to secure the making of laws to promote personal freedom; that as soon as it can be done, I shall legally set free all those under my care; and that, in the meantime, I shall treat them with kindness and equity, it being my constant aim to act upon the command of the Lord Jesus Christ, to do unto others as I would wish them to do unto me.[50]

For this, King Eyo earned himself Waddell's estimation as a strong conservative who wished all reform to proceed from himself and conceded "cautiously and sparingly and only with universal consent."[51]

In this Waddell appears to have been quite oblivious to the fact that he, together will all the members of SAISC, was a reformer who wished all reform to proceed from himself and at a pace that he wished it to happen. The consent of the Africans who were supposed to be undergoing this transformation was largely irrelevant and not sought for. When the opinion of Africans was contrary, the members of the SAISC were able to marshal the clout of the Consul in Fernando Po and the naval squadron and bring it to bear on the Ekpe.[52] The Rev. Hugh Goldie, the key person in the translation of the Efik New Testament, arrived on this scene in June 1847 and, in 1858, upon the departure of Waddell from Old Calabar, took charge of Creek Town.[53]

---

50. Dickie, *Story of the Mission in Old Calabar*, 51–52.

51. Waddell, entry for 1 Jan. 1851, *Journals*, vol. VIII, 105.

52. See Anderson, Journal extracts in *Missionary Record*, 1850, 105–10, entry for Friday, 8 Feb.; Waddell, entry for 15 Feb. 1851, *Journals*, vol. VII, 157.

53. Dickie, *Story of the Mission in Old Calabar*, 29–30, 56.

5

Language and Translation Work

Education was at the centre of both the intentions of the missionaries and the aspirations of the Calabarese, as evident in the exchanges leading to the establishment of the mission.[1] However, given the upper hand in ability to enforce judgements that the missionaries increasingly enjoyed, there was little likelihood, if any, that the Africans would be able to ensure that the education given by mission schools was in keeping with their specifications. The chiefs of Bonny, for instance, went as far as specifying what sort of education they wanted for their children. They did not want religious teaching as the children already had that. Rather, they wanted them "to be taught how to gauge palm-oil and the other mercantile business as soon as possible."[2]

Therefore, in keeping with the prescriptions of the missionaries, the civilizing and evangelizing mandates, not trade, became the foundations for the education offered. The best that the African rulers could do was to personally reject the gospel. We have already noted how not even the incredibly accommodating King Eyo Honesty II had embraced Christianity by the time he died.

Ajayi records the minor concessions to reform that the rulers were willing to make in their pursuit of an education for their children. These included forbidding Sunday markets and putting a ban on drumming near churches on Sunday. But accepting baptism was out of the question. More serious reform like the prohibition of human sacrifice, the killing of twin babies, trial by ordeal

---

1. Education featured prominently in the published request from the African rulers of Bonny to Liverpool in 1848, the letters from King Eyamba and Seven Chiefs in 1842, and in the letter from King Eyo Honesty II of Creek Town. Goldie, *Calabar and its Mission*, 73–75.

2. Crowther, "Brief Statements exhibiting the characters, habits and ideas of the Natives of the Bight," 1874; C.M.S. CA3/04. Cited in Ajayi, *Christian Missions in Nigeria*, 133.

and the right of the Mission House to provide asylum for runaway slaves had to be enacted under duress and enforced by the Consul with the help of the navy.³

In keeping with Buxton's *Prospectus of the Society for the Extinction of the Slave Trade and the Civilization of Africa*, reducing the principal languages of Western Africa into writing was a priority.⁴ Waddell started collecting a list of Efik words from the Liverpool supercargoes and began to memorize them and try to simplify and systematize their orthography even before he set out for Calabar. These studies resulted in the publication of the *Vocabulary of the Efik Language* in 1849.⁵

The choice of Efik as the language of translation was made because Efik was understood by all the societies of the area as evidenced by Nida's note of 1972:

> Efik is spoken with tribal dialectical differences by more than 1.2 million people in Calabar Province of Nigeria. Numerous tribes, collectively known as Ibibio (Anang, Andone, Eket, Enyong, and Efik) speak related dialects, of which Efik is the accepted literary form and the one used in education. The Ibibio tongues form a dialect cluster within the Benue-Congo language group.⁶

No doubt, Waddell and his colleagues were well advised in this choice of language by the Liverpool supercargoes and some of the other Europeans who had had some contact with the area.⁷

The pioneering nature of reducing Efik into writing was a daunting undertaking by any standards. In the words of Goldie, whose scholarly capabilities soon established him as the authority on Efik in Calabar:⁸

> To the philologist the languages of the Ethiopia races present much the same *terra incognita* as the regions which they cover do to the geographer, and the latter will get the desideratum of his science supplied in the exploration of the African continent before the

---

3. Ajayi, *Christian Missions in Nigeria*, 65, 100.

4. *The African Slave Trade and its Remedy*, 8–16.

5. Ajayi, *Christian Missions in Nigeria*, 130–31. See also H. M. Waddell, *A Vocabulary of the Efik or Old Calabar Language: with prayers and lessons*. Edinburgh: Grant and Taylor, 1849.

6. E. A. Nida, ed., *The Book of a Thousand Tongues*, rev. ed. (London: United Bible Societies, 1972), 114. Obviously, the status of Efik as "the accepted literary form and the one used in education" is one it attained following the work done by missionaries to reduce it into writing and to prepare grammars for it.

7. An example of the latter is a certain Dr. Fergusson who had some experience as a surgeon in West Africa and was consulted by the missionaries during the planning stage of the mission. Ajayi, *Christian Missions in Nigeria*, 45.

8. Ajayi, *Christian Missions in Nigeria*, 130.

former succeeds in filling up the *hiatus* in his by the acquirement of the knowledge of its tongues.[9]

Smalley puts the task in perspective when he notes that translators have to cope with vast time and cultural distance, incompatibility of literary styles, and greater differences in linguistic structure.[10] In this case, the missionary had to cope with these issues with respect to the biblical texts, his own epistemological world and that of the Calabarese. These three worlds represent the three strata that needed to be accessed and, having been accessed, related to each other to ensure fidelity to the message of the Bible in all the three epistemological worlds. In the words of Smalley, "the degree to which a translation makes the original message accessible is also the measure of that translation."[11]

In retrospect, and from the perspective of fidelity in the transmission of meaning cross-culturally, this task was further complicated by the one-sided nature of the process of collecting linguistic data and creating orthography for the Efik. The missionary, starting with Waddell prior to the entrance of the mission, was in control of this process, to the practical exclusion of direct input by the native Calabarese. To borrow Kwesi Dickson's phrase, this control entailed that epistemological "exclusivism" was at the centre of the process.[12]

It is the case, then, that the orthography and grammar of Efik were created using preconceived assumptions about the principles which governed Efik. Further, these preconceived assumptions were those of the missionary and, by extension, of his Indo-European epistemological constitution. For Goldie, this was in spite of his own confession that in forming their vocables from the root of the verb, in idiom, and in grammatical structure, African languages appeared to be more closely allied to the Semitic than to the Indo-European languages.[13]

However, within this "exclusivist" model, individual missionaries differed from each other in the degree to which they understood the complexity of

---

9. Goldie, *Calabar and its Mission*, 299. See also his own introduction to *Efik Grammar and Dictionary* (Glasgow, 1862; reprint, Edinburgh, 1874).

10. *Translation and Mission*, 2.

11. *Translation and Mission*, 2.

12. "What does not seem to have sufficiently engaged the attention of the church is the possibility of a convert's humanity being distorted in the attempt to achieve conformity with the institutional specifications with respect to the style of church membership, interpreting the Bible, proclaiming the gospel message, and so forth." K. A. Dickson, *Uncompleted Mission: Christianity and Exclusivism* (Maryknoll: Orbis Books, 1991), ix. We have already seen how the understanding that grammar, as the science of words and the art of employing words according to the established usage of a language, was perceived by Goldie to obey the same principles in all languages. Goldie, *Principles of Efik Grammar*, 13.

13. Goldie, *Calabar and its Mission*, 301–302.

the task and sought to go about minimizing their losses in fidelity to the message. The degree to which this complexity was appreciated is reflected by the point made earlier that missionaries were not, in the vast majority of cases, selected for their potential as Bible translators.[14] For the Calabar Mission, this is borne out by the fact that it was Waddell, a man whose strengths lay in his deep and practical spirituality and the ability to inspire others, and not in scholarly and literary acumen,[15] who was chosen by his peers to head the pioneering party.[16] Dickie calls Waddell the "William Carey of the movement" as a tribute to his passion and drive to rally others to see the mission make the transition from vision to fruition. For "men are emboldened by the bold."[17] He extols "his statesmanlike sagacity and philanthropic purpose" and credits him with shaping:

> the destiny of our African mission at a time when mission work in Africa was little known. His book on the *Twenty-nine Years in the West Indies and Central Africa* is a worthy monument of his indefatigable labour – a brilliant and first-hand record of his interesting experiences in Old Calabar, which will take its place beside the works of Livingstone, Moffat and Stanley.[18]

In evaluating the missionaries of the early fifties in Calabar, he credits Waddell with "zeal and spirituality" and Goldie with "scholarly tastes and calm perseverance."[19]

Those who were keenly aware of the complexity of the task tried to compensate by undertaking time to study the coefficients of translation. They also, to varying degrees, undertook extensive consultations with what amounted to "native sounding boards"[20] before publishing anything.

Lists of published language and Bible translation works before the close of the nineteenth-century show, predictably, that a lot of people tried their hand at Bible translation and translating educational aids. These include the Efik New Testament by Hugh Goldie (1862); Genesis by Hugh Goldie (1862); the Psalter by Hugh Goldie (1866); Proverbs by W. Anderson (1866); the Old Testament by Alexander Robb, with the assistance of Esien Esien and other

---

14. Smalley, *Translation and Mission*, 16.
15. Ajayi, *Christian Missions in Nigeria*, 130.
16. Dickie, *Story of the Mission in Old Calabar*, 13.
17. Dickie, *Story of the Mission in Old Calabar*, 10, 12.
18. Dickie, *Story of the Mission in Old Calabar*, 55–56.
19. Dickie, *Story of the Mission of Old Calabar*, 45.
20. Smalley, *Translation and Mission*, 15.

natives (1868); Jonah by an unknown translator (1850); John (1852), Romans (1857), a revision of John (1858), and 1 John (1858) all translated between William Anderson, Hugh Goldie and Hope Waddell with the assistance of Aye Eyo and others. They also include John by William Anderson, with the help of Hugh Goldie and Hope Waddell (1852), extracts from 1 and 2 Kings, Jonah, a Meditation and Prayer (1853), a selection of Scripture verses grouped together under subjects in Efik and English (1853), a selection of 28 hymns in Efik, the Shorter Catechism by William Anderson (1856); Romans and portions of 1 Corinthians by William Anderson (1857); and 1 John by Hope Waddell (1858).[21]

Samuel Edgerley, the printer, was a part of the 1849 *Vocabulary of the Efik Language* project.[22] When William Jameson joined the mission in February 1847, which time, given the retreat to Fernando Po that the missionaries made in October 1846 in order to escape the "smokes,"[23] represented a period of six months since the entrance of the mission:

> Two schools had been opened, a printing press had been erected, two school books had been printed, an Efik vocabulary of nearly three thousand words had been lithographed and the natives had heard the gospel preached and seen it lived at their very doors.[24]

However, it was with the arrival of Hugh Goldie in June 1847 that translation work gathered momentum:

> Mr. Goldie soon mastered the language, and composed a catechism in Efik and English, four hundred copies of which were printed in Old Calabar within about a year. He also got the Ten Commandments printed in Efik on broad sheets, and hung them up in the houses. The older boys in the schools soon were able to read the Bible, passages of which were translated by Mr. Goldie. The work done within about three years may be indicated by the

---

21. *Historical Catalogue of the Printed Editions of Holy Scripture in the Library of the British and Foreign Bible Society*, vol. II, 1; *Polyglots and Languages Other than English*, compiled by T. H. Darlow and H. F. Moule (London, 1903; reprint New York: Kraus Reprint Corporation, 1963), 335–36; Nida, *The Book of a Thousand Tongues*, 114–15; and G. E. Coldham, comp., *African Scriptures*, vol. 1, *A Bibliography of Scriptures in African Languages* (London: The British and Foreign Bible Society, 1966), 135–40. Obviously, most of these works were produced by more than one missionary and the credits do not necessarily reflect the levels of input by those who were involved.
22. Ajayi, *Christian Missions in Nigeria*, 131.
23. This was the name given to the dry or hazy season in Calabar.
24. Dickie, *Story of the Mission in Old Calabar*, 26–27.

fact that during that time Mr. Edgerley had thrown off from his printing-press 55,300 pages for the enlightenment of Old Calabar.²⁵

Goldie was the key man in translation work at this young mission. However, if the Foreign Missions Committee had had its way, this portfolio would have fallen to Dr. Robb of Aberdeen, a brilliant scholar and famous for his Hebrew, who was specifically brought in to "prosecute more energetically the work of translation and Efik orthography." Yet, after publishing his translations from the Old Testament in 1866, health reasons led to his transfer to Jamaica, leaving the less-educated Goldie to carry the mantle of scholar in Calabar.²⁶

Goldie

> published in 1862 his *Principles of Efik Grammar and Specimens of the Language*, and translations from the New Testament into Efik the following year . . . Goldie's ability blossomed out. In 1874 he published the *Efik Dictionary*, the *Efik Grammar in Efik* and the *Efik Grammar in English*. These works dominated the studies of other missionaries, who produced translations, primers, readers, hymns and sermons; and indeed to this day they remain the standard works on the language.²⁷

He was the main translator of the Efik New Testament that we will focus on in the next major section.²⁸ It is, therefore, necessary to consider his theory of language and translation in some detail.

---

25. Dickie, *Story of the Mission in Old Calabar*, 33.
26. Ajayi, *Christian Missions in Nigeria*, 131.
27. Ajayi, *Christian Missions in Nigeria*, 131.
28. The entry in the *Historical Catalogue of the Printed Editions of Scripture* indicates that he "availed himself of a translation of St. John's Gospel, Romans and Hebrews, with portions of other books, already prepared by his colleague W. Anderson," although it is not clear whether these had been printed at the mission press, or existed only in MS (335).

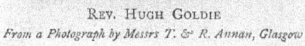

Figure 2. The Rev. Hugh Goldie and Rev. S. H. Edgerly, Old Calabar Mission.[29]

Goldie's Theory of Language and Translation

To a very large extent, Goldie owes his success and reputation as the scholar in Calabar to his awareness of the challenges of coming to terms with the languages of the so-called Ethiopian races. "Ethiopia" was, apparently, a term often used to represent native Africans.[30] Therefore, an outbreak of divine consciousness for "Ethiopia" among the Jamaica presbytery led to the Mission to Calabar. Goldie's sensitivity to these challenges extended to his feel for the entire field of linguistic studies. He was well acquainted with the chief authorities on intertropical African languages in English in his time:

> Koelle, whose *Polyglotta Africana* is a work of great industry, but unavoidably very inaccurate; Prichard's *History of Man*; Bunsein's *Egypt*; Latham's Papers contributed to the British Association for the Advancement of Science, which were epitomized afterwards in his *Comparative Philology*; Dr. Cust's *Sketch of the Modern Languages of Africa*. The last-named work very much supersedes

---

29. H. Goldie, *Calabar and its Mission: With additional chapters by Rev. John Taylor Dean* (Edinburgh and London: Oliphant, Anderson & Ferrier, 1901), 251.

30. Dickie, *Story of the Mission in Old Calabar*, 10–11.

all the former, and has been the work of vast industry, such only as one who has a talent for and love of philology would undertake.[31]

Not surprisingly, Goldie adopted the work of Cust, a scholar keenly aware of the tentative nature of his own work, as the foundation for his research.[32] From Goldie's defence of Cust's work, it is clear that the reason for Cust's self-deprecation was the rapid pace at which discoveries in Africa were making conclusions in philology obsolete. Yet, to Goldie, the value of Cust's work lay in its invaluable use as a treatment of the subject to the point to which it had advanced up to that time.[33] In keeping with Cust, therefore, Goldie follows the classification of African languages devised by F. Müller: "I. Semitic; II. Hamitic; III. Nubu Fulah; IV. Negro; V. Bantu; VI. Hottentont-Bushmen; It is with the fourth division we have to do in speaking of the Efik language."[34]

The common understanding of the time was that there was

> such a difference of the language of the tribes of the south of the equator from that of the northern tribes as to call for their division into two distinct families; and that those of the south so much resemble each other, that they all may be classified under one head, named the Bantu.[35]

The geographical line of demarcation between these allegedly different families was the river Rio del Rey, in the Kameroons mountain range, so that Efik occupies the borderland.

However, this is a distinction that Goldie questions on the grounds that Efik, one of the northern tongues, "forms by far the greater part of its vocables, as the Semitic does, from the root of the verb; and though the alliteral or euphonic concord be carried out more systematically in [southern tongues], we find the law obtaining more or less in [northern tongues]."[36] This proves, for Goldie, that "there is no such marked line of demarcation between the languages of the northern and southern tribes." In fact, in keeping with Bleek's Comparative Grammar, he suspects that most of the Negro languages of West Africa are connected with the Bantu family, with a West African division of

---

31. Goldie, *Calabar and its Mission*, 299–300.
32. R. N. Cust, *A Sketch of the Modern Languages of Africa: Accompanied by a Language Map*, vol. I (London: Trubner, 1883), 56. In Cust's own estimation of his work, it was utterly worthless.
33. Goldie, *Calabar and its Mission*, 300.
34. Goldie, *Calabar and its Mission*, 300.
35. Goldie, *Calabar and its Mission*, 300.
36. Goldie, *Calabar and its Mission*, 301.

the Bantu family extending from the Kameroons mountains to Sierra Leone, "which share[s] the peculiarities of euphonic and novel harmonic laws."[37] His suspicions are largely borne out by Mbiti for whom the main linguistic groups are: "Bantu, found in eastern, central and southern Africa, and extending westwards up to the Cameroons; Hamitio-Semitic, found in the south-eastern and northern Africa; Khoisan, in southern Africa; Malayo-Polynesian, on the island of Madagascar; Nigritic, in Western Africa; and Sudanic, in the Sudan region stretching westwards."[38]

Further, for Goldie, it is a connection that is more marked in their idiom than in their vocabularies or grammatical form. It is essentially one, and so claims for them a common parentage:

> As our knowledge of them extends, it is found that they are in this as well as in grammatical structure more closely allied to the Semitic than to the Indo-European tongues. Not only in the idiom of their languages, but also in the usage of everyday life, the descendants of Ham have kept more closely connected with those of Shem than the family of Japhet have with either.[39]

In seeing affinities between the southern tongues and the northern tongues that are deeper-seated than vocabularies and grammatical forms, thereby suggesting a common parentage for both, Goldie made the connection with the epistemological constitution that, I have argued elsewhere, stands behind African languages.[40]

On the other hand, in seeing that in these affinities as well as in grammatical structure, African languages are more closely allied to the Semitic than to the Indo-European languages, Goldie made the connection between this epistemological construct and the Semitic epistemological construct.[41] The African epistemological constitution bears striking parallels

---

37. Goldie, *Calabar and its Mission*, 301.
38. Mbiti, *African Religions & Philosophy*, 101.
39. Goldie, *Calabar and its Mission*, 302.
40. Nyirenda, "Epistemological Hegemony in the History of Christianity." The hypothesis there was that the essence of Africanness for modern Africans is to be found in their mental universe or epistemological constitution. This, as the foundation which informs cultural particularities such as language, beliefs and social structures, is sufficiently homogenous in Sub-Saharan Africa to be adopted as the basis on which indigenous originality and agency in mission can be measured and built. See also W. A. Dyrness, *Learning about Theology from the Third World* (Grand Rapids, Michigan: Zondervan, 1990), 42.
41. In M. Nyirenda, "A Critical Review of the Nature and Extent of the Discussion concerning Hebrewisms in African Cultures," MTh. (R) Paper II, CSCNWW, University of Edinburgh, June 2001, I have shown that the affinities between African and Semitic cultures

with its Semitic counterpart that need to be exploited for an African biblical hermeneutical method.

It is highly significant that, in spite of his awareness of the epistemological distance between his Indo-European world view and both the African and Semitic world views, Goldie proceeded to reduce the Efik into writing using "standard" principles of grammar and an Indo-European orthographical template:

> In reducing to writing an unwritten tongue, the Roman alphabet is, I suppose, universally employed, so far as is required; and when new sounds have to be represented, and also to distinguish sounds confused by our English orthography, a new character should be employed, so that each character may have one unvarying sound.[42]

Therefore, beginning with an Indo-European epistemological framework – the Roman alphabet and its symbolism in European languages – the Efik language was reduced to writing. This meant that the missionary was making choices about representing what were very concrete realities spanning generations of development in the speech, thought and meaning structure of the Calabarese, with literary symbols that already had histories of meanings, sounds, and usage in Indo-European contexts. Given the pioneering nature of this task, and the multiplicity of its protagonists, it is hardly surprising that uniformity in symbol quickly became a matter of dispute.[43]

To resolve this dispute, some philologists suggested adopting a uniform alphabet for all unwritten languages.[44] It was not adopted universally:

> At the instance of the directors of missionary societies whose work was carried on among unlettered tribes, the eminent philologist, Dr. Lepsius, produced a scheme of a uniform alphabet, which was approved of, and has to a certain extent been a guide to

---

cannot be convincingly shown to derive from a common parentage. I also argued that this does not mean that Africans cannot gain by exploiting the affinities that are observable for their approach to biblical studies.

42. Goldie, *Calabar and its Mission*, 302–303.

43. Goldie, *Calabar and its Mission*, 303.

44. "The scheme of a uniform alphabet has been frequently proposed by philologists, and the adoption of such in the case of unwritten languages would be comparatively easy, as it is most desirable, especially when different missions are labouring in the same language." Goldie, *Calabar and its Mission*, 303.

missionaries in the West of Africa, for whom it was provided, but has not been implicitly followed.⁴⁵

However, for the purposes of our discussion, it must be noted that this discussion was among European philologists and missionaries. Africans could not participate in this discussion in as much as the protagonists of mission and the civilizing mandate were Europeans.

Fundamentally, then, the very project of reducing African languages to writing, and linking their orthographies to existing orthographies, was outside the scope of Africans. The Calabarese understandably lacked both the skills and the vision to do so and could scarcely be expected to contest the choices that went into reducing the Efik into writing.⁴⁶

Thus, we find that, in the very noble task of bridging the communication divide between Africans and the entire legacy of Western knowledge and experience, including its understanding of Christianity, we already see elements of hegemony. The very literary vehicles that were established to carry the weight of generations of meaning, thought, and its communication in verbal and non-verbal symbolism were given to Africans by people who could scarcely grasp the African realities they sought to capture in writing.

In retrospect, this was the beginning of, among other things, a radical imposition of an Indo-European epistemological paradigm on an African one. The educational mandate as a tool for both passing on Western forms of knowledge to Africans largely at the expense of African forms of knowledge, and reshaping the consciousness of Africans, was underway.⁴⁷ The foundational and enduring nature of these pioneer language works is self-evident everywhere that missionaries had to reduce the language of the natives to writing.⁴⁸ In other words, in the matter of creating a link between their intellectual and spiritual reality and literature, Africans, unlike other societies elsewhere, did not have the opportunity of creatively and dynamically, over time, developing their

---

45. Goldie, *Calabar and its Mission*, 303–304. See also R. Lepsius, *Standard Alphabet for Reducing Unwritten Languages and Foreign Graphic Systems to a Uniform Orthography in European Letters*, 2nd ed. (London: Williams and Norgate, 1863).

46. Among the missionaries, though, it was a contentious matter. By way of illustration, the NT and Psalms of the Bechuana language by the London Missionary Society was found incomprehensible to French missionaries working among the same people because the latter were using a different orthography. Lepsius, *System of Universal Orthography*, 7. For Lepsius, this, no doubt, underscored the need for a uniform alphabet.

47. See Wa Thiong'o, *Decolonising the Mind*.

48. See Ajayi, *Christian Missions in Nigeria*, xv, 131.

own orthography, but were gifted with orthographies by those who sought to understand them.[49]

Goldie and others like him "mastered" the vernacular languages and embarked on the work of translating the Scriptures and writing books for use in school and church. Portions of Scripture were put out as soon as "sufficient mastery" was attained of the language of the people, as soon as "they could use them sufficiently to reveal the great scheme of mercy in Christ, and instruct in the way of life."[50]

This was a pragmatic decision and the ability to establish any form of communication of the gospel was the overriding factor. However, when he undertook the translation of the New Testament, Goldie had fidelity in mind: "we thought it well to secure the great body of the language before undertaking the work of strict translation."[51] This entailed taking sixteen years from the entrance of the mission to the publication of his 1862 New Testament. Yet, even with this level of care, he prefaced his work with a disclaimer:

> The Efik being but in process of formation as a written medium of thought, nothing we now produce will be permanent. The present translation will, therefore, attain its ultimate purpose in laying the foundation of something more perfect; and while it serves its day, may God the Holy Ghost graciously condescend to employ it as a means of scattering abundantly the seed of Divine Truth amidst the heathenism of Old Calabar, and of turning many from darkness to light.[52]

Part of Goldie's challenge was to try to translate, using orthographies indebted to the Indo-European epistemological constitution, a message couched in terms and forms bearing greater idiomatic affinity with the Efik than with English.[53] How he tried to bridge this gap is the subject of the next chapter.

---

49. For an example of how this process looks like when a society has the liberty to borrow, shape and develop their own way of writing, and how this captures their world of reality, see Moshe Greenberg, *Introduction to Hebrew*, Englewood Cliffs, New Jersey: Prentice-Hall, Inc., 1964.

50. Goldie, *Calabar and its Mission*, 304, note.

51. Goldie, *Calabar and its Mission*, 304, note.

52. *Obufa Testament: Abon Ye Andinyana Nyin Jisus Krist* (Edinburgh: Murray Ye Gibb, 1862), 2.

53. Goldie, *Calabar and its Mission*, 304.

6

Translation and Translators

Our concern in this chapter is to ascertain, as much as possible, the identities of the people involved in the translation of the Efik New Testament and the roles that they played in that process. In the absence of detailed accounts and original material, as is the case for Laws, we will rely on circumstantial evidence to make our case.[1]

We are already aware of the apparent interaction and consultation that translators enjoyed within Calabar.[2] We are also aware of Goldie's use of translations of St. John's Gospel, Romans and Hebrews, with portions of other books, already prepared by his colleague W. Anderson.[3]

However, despite the qualifications above, we can still proceed with the understanding that Goldie was the chief translator, redactor and compiler of the Efik New Testament. It is, therefore, useful to try to determine how he went about the task of translation.

The Resources Used in the Translation

The resources available for this project may be divided into two categories: implicit and specific resources. In keeping with the understanding that these translations were multi-interactive and multi-consultative works, we may, to a point, safely assume that Waddell's work was available for Goldie's use. This

---

1. To the best of my knowledge, Goldie did not keep an account of his translation projects. He did, however, make several references to them that provide a reasonable picture of what was obtaining.

2. As an illustration, the note in Nida, *The Book of a Thousand Tongues*, 115, shows John (1852), Romans (1857), a revision of John (1858), and 1 John (1858), as "all translated between William Anderson, Hugh Goldie and Hope Waddell with the assistance of Aye Eyo and others."

3. *Historical Catalogue of the Printed Editions of Scripture*, 335.

must have included the memorized, simplified and systematized orthography of Efik words published as the *Vocabulary of the Efik Language*.[4]

Goldie's research concluded that Efik was a northern language that forms the greater part of its vocables from the root of the verb.[5] He also speculated that the idiomatic nature of African languages suggests a common parentage.[6] From the above, we may deduce that he undertook thorough and substantial primary research. We may also deduce that he did this while consulting studies done by authorities on intertropical African languages in English.[7] In fact, it is this research that led him to publish *Principles of Efik Grammar and Specimens of Language* (1862), the *Efik Dictionary* (1874), *Efik Grammar in Efik* (1874) and *Efik Grammar in English* (1874), not to mention the *Efik New Testament* (1862).

He provides evidence of some of the specific resources that he used in the preface to his translation. The text he translated was that of Dr. Bloomfield:

> I have deemed it would be unjustifiable to throw aside all that has been gained by the labours of the learned, since the publication of the Elzevir edition, towards the securing of a correct text; and as I had no pretensions to be a judge in such matters, I took the revision which differs least from the Vulgate Greek, in which no alteration is made except as may be held to be universally received. A few readings are adopted from Alford, on the side of which the evidence of MSS decidedly preponderated, or which, in the case of equipoise, the Efik could most accurately express.[8]

In addition to these primary choices, he had recourse to other apparatus: "The Latin Vulgate, Beza's version, the Authorized English translation, with the versions and commentaries of Calvin, Doddridge, Campbell, and MacKnight, were made use of, and Bengel's Gnomon. Stuart's and Eadie's Commentaries were also consulted on the portions of Scripture they embrace."[9] The works of Anderson above are supplemented with "portions of several other books, which have been of material assistance in the preparation of this version."[10] It is, however, difficult to judge the exact nature of this "material assistance."

---

4. Ajayi, *Christian Missions in Nigeria*, 130–31.
5. Goldie, *Calabar and its Mission*, 301.
6. Goldie, *Calabar and its Mission*, 302.
7. Goldie, *Calabar and its Mission*, 299–300.
8. Goldie, *Efik New Testament*, 1.
9. Goldie, *The Efik New Testament*, 2.
10. Goldie, *The Efik New Testament*, 1.

From the above, there can be no doubt that Goldie was unusually motivated to familiarize himself with the best, as far as access permitted, of scholarly tools and the efforts of his colleagues in Calabar. It must be noted, however, that if at all there was any doubt before, it is now clear that, in the matter of access to the text of translation, Goldie was answerable to his own judgements. Therefore, in the selection of texts and in the justification of these selections, Goldie stood alone. Likewise, in the adoption of textual choices between variant readings, he stood alone.

The Translator(s) and their Roles

As we saw in the previous subsection, it is quite clear that Goldie was in total control of the decisions relating to the biblical texts. Likewise, he was in control of determining the secondary apparatus consulted in the course of the translation. In epistemological terms, this represents methodologically exclusive choices of accessibility to the biblical message by an Indo-European cleric, using tools that belong to the same tradition.

Ernst E. Wendland calls this initial accessibility the message transmission event that involves the "primary, or original, event which produced the text in the source language."[11] This was the epistemological apparatus that was decisive in his choice of revisions that differed least from the "Vulgate Greek" (sic.) and only included such alterations as may have been "held to be universally received."[12]

Ian Maxwell has shown how Alexander Duff, the first Church of Scotland missionary, was a product of nineteenth-century Scotland Enlightenment sensibilities and how this influenced him to advocate a specific educational agenda in Calcutta. In this agenda, "it is the Enlightenment conviction that learning, or education has a key role in the emergence and development of civil society" that was its guiding premise. But this was a British education, not just any other education.

> What was necessary, Duff insisted, was the prior Western rationality, which provided the framework necessary to grasp the significance of the "evidences" [a vast body of apologetic theology whereby existing rational objections to Christianity of

---

11. Ernst E. Wendland, *The Cultural Factor in Bible Translation: A Study of Communicating the Word of God in a Central African Cultural Context*, UBS Monograph Series, No. 2 (London, New York, Stuttgart: United Bible Societies, 1987), 17.

12. Goldie, *Efik New Testament*, 1. He probably meant "Koine Greek."

every conceivable approach, style, and content, were analysed methodically and systematically refuted, and non-existent rational objections anticipated and headed off at the pass] ... Western rationality had an obvious and destructive impact on the sacredness of the Hindu Shasters. If, he announced, "you only impart ordinary useful knowledge, you thereby demolish what by its people is regarded as sacred."[13]

It is not far-fetched to assume that Goldie's epistemological choices were governed by the same sensibilities although, in Goldie's case, the sensibilities were indirect and without conscious intent. It is only after translation that he "for the most part" read it to Aye Eyo (John Eyo), whom he considered the best authority on the Efik language; and the parts that Goldie did not read with Eyo he revised with other natives "competent to give a judgement as regards their own tongue." Yet, he was aware that they "could not, of course, judge of the correctness of the translation." They could only say whether it was written in correct Efik.[14]

No doubt, this was of great help to Goldie's efforts at making a translation that is comprehensible to Efik-speaking Calabarese. Towards this end, he also enlisted the assistance of Messrs Anderson, Robb and Thomson for corrections and suggestions.[15]

In the end, the Efik New Testament was a one-man translation, albeit one man who consulted widely. With respect to biblical text, he had the input of fellow Scottish Presbyterian missionaries who were available, with Robb most likely being the person who could help most. With respect to the Efik, some Calabarese had an opportunity to give their opinions about the comprehensibility of the Efik renderings. The Efik New Testament was bound together with Goldie's translation of Genesis.

This translation is one of the inspiring stories of the Old Calabar Mission. Apparently,

> When the recently freed slaves of the West Indies heard that Scriptures were being prepared for the Calabar region, where most of the Jamaican slaves and their forebears had been taken into bondage, it was decided that they would contribute to the

---

13. "Alexander Duff and the General Assembly's Institution in Calcutta, 1830 to 1840." Paper presented at New College, University of Edinburgh on 26 June 2001.

14. Goldie, *Efik New Testament*, 2.

15. Goldie, *Efik New Testament*, 2.

evangelization of their African kinsmen. Thus, out of their penury, these freedmen saved enough to finance the translation and printing of the Efik Genesis.[16]

The Mission Church at New Broughton, Jamaica, under the pastoral care of the Rev. Andrew Gordon Hogg, was the congregation behind the project.[17] Its novelty lay in the notion that, coming from a mission church, it represented second-generation fruit of mission.[18]

Time Frame and its Relation to the Circumstances of the Project

We noted above that Goldie had fidelity, not merely pragmatic function, in mind when he translated the Efik New Testament. We also noted how, towards this end, he endeavoured to "secure the great body of the language before undertaking the work of strict translation."

Since Goldie arrived in Calabar in June 1847, it means that he took fourteen years[19] to translate the Efik New Testament. That, in itself, bespeaks commitment to very high standards of scholarship that he set upon himself. The fact that he simultaneously published the Efik New Testament and *Principles of Efik Grammar and Specimens of the Language* shows that this translation was done in the light of all his work in Efik grammar up to that point.

However, this obviously very judiciously undertaken piece of work was still a product of Goldie's Enlightenment-inspired epistemological choices. Whatever vestige of Calabarese epistemological constitution it may contain was processed through Goldie. In the absence of a direct analysis of the text of the Efik New Testament, it is still possible to discern, from the fragmentary evidence of the process, the quality of this translation. In spite of the unusual care, it is, at best, a functional and not linguistically precise translation, as the translator admits in the preface. It is also a foundational piece of work for subsequent attempts at translation into the Efik.

---

16. Nida, *Book of a Thousand Tongues*, 114.

17. *Historical Catalogue of the Printed Editions of Scripture*, 336.

18. F. Knight, "The History of the National Bible Society of Scotland" (Unpublished Research Work, Edinburgh, The National Bible Society of Scotland, 1937?), 159–61. See also the Preface to W. C. Somerville, *From Iona to Dunblane: The Story of the National Bible Society of Scotland to 1948* (Edinburgh: The National Bible Society of Scotland, 1948).

19. The completed manuscript of the Efik New Testament was submitted to the National Bible Society of Scotland for Publication in October 1861. Knight, "The History of the National Bible Society of Scotland," 160–61.

7

The Immediate Impact of the Translation on the Calabarese

The immediate impact of the Efik New Testament must be examined in the context of the impact of other translation work of the time.

Dickie alludes to what must have been a wide-ranging phenomenon at the time when missionaries were very dependent on interpreters. It was not uncommon, he notes, for an interpreter to take the liberty of adding or subtracting from the message in rendering the speaker's thoughts into Efik.[1] On the other hand, King Eyo Honesty II was known to constructively criticize Waddell's sermons after interpreting for him.[2] This could account for some of the additions and subtractions. These interpreters were able to assume this role because they already spoke English.[3]

Given the lack of ready converts,[4] for a while, the force of translation work was directed at the mission schools. Bible passages were part of the reading texts[5] and were probably incorporated in the material for primers and readers:

> The driving force behind the work in Nigerian languages was the anxiety to teach the converts and would-be converts to read

---

1. Dickie, *Story of the Mission in Old Calabar*, 19.

2. Ajayi, *Christian Missions in Nigeria*, 101. One such criticism was his advice to Waddell to preach on first principles of religion as a preparation for the gospel. Such discussions apparently deepened Waddell's respect for King Eyo.

3. Ajayi, *Christian Missions in Nigeria*, 100.

4. After three years of work, there was no convert in Calabar. Ironically, it was the unconverted King Eyo who consoled a discouraged Waddell by reminding him that in spite of the word of God being preached in England for the preceding one thousand years, many did not believe and obey it. Ajayi, *Christian Missions in Nigeria*, 101. The first convert was Esien Esien Ukpabio, a slave, in 1853, six years after the entrance of the mission. Dickie, *Story of the Mission in Old Calabar*, 46.

5. Dickie, *Story of the Mission in Old Calabar*, 33.

the Bible in them . . . Indeed, the strong evangelical influence in the missionary movement placed great premium on the Sabbath school for teaching adult converts and catechumens who could not come to school daily during the week to read the New Testament for themselves. It was especially for their sake that so much emphasis was placed on translating the Bible into vernaculars; for their sake, too that throughout the work on languages the emphasis was on simplicity of orthography rather than academic perfection.[6]

In this educational programme there was, therefore, a meeting of agendas. The missionaries sought to impart the gospel while civilizing the young and old. This specifically fuelled translation work. The Calabarese, on the other hand, had little interest in or use for the vernacular. They were more interested in the sort of learning that would influence their economic development. Ajayi notes that the Calabarese would have thought little of a school that did not attempt to teach some English:

> The missionaries welcomed this demand such as it was. They knew that it was one of the principle reasons they were welcomed and allowed to settle in the city-states on the coast. They saw in schools "the nursery of the infant church," the principal hope for the success of their work. If most of the adults were too much wedded to the ideas of their fathers, the children, whose minds were as yet unhardened, should provide more fruitful ground for the sowing of the seed of the new religion . . . Let the children come to school for any purpose whatever and it would be the fault of the missionary if he could not take advantage of the opportunity and make Christian converts of the children.[7]

After the publication of the Efik New Testament, there is a record of the appreciation of the native Calabarese:

---

6. Ajayi, *Christian Missions in Nigeria*, 131. The adult literacy classes in particular focused on reading the Bible, the Catechism (setting out basic doctrine), and some hymns (132).

7. *Christian Missions in Nigeria*, 134. Apparently, this was a position adopted after being disillusioned at the prospects of converting adults. See J. M. Harden, 4 May 1858, to Poindexter, *The Commission*, July 1858: "Brethren, I tell you again that I have *no* hope of the parents; my hope is in their children"; R. H. Stone to Culpepper, 9 July 1858: "I am fast coming to the conviction that *schools for the rising generation* must be the *basis* of all missions among *barbarous* and *savage* heathen. The Gospel should be preached regularly and steadily, faithfully and prayerfully; but through the children we get at the root of idolatry and leaven the whole lump." Cited in Ajayi, *Christian Missions in Nigeria*, 134.

> A first edition of 500 copies . . . of the Efik Testament was . . . dispatched to Calabar. It was the first version in a hitherto unknown tongue which the N.B.S.S. had published. A touching letter of thanks from the natives was received, written by Esien Esien Ukpabio, the first and oldest convert.[8]

However, Esien Esien's letter would hardly represent popular Calabarese sentiment because, being a slave, he was the sort of native that stood to gain from the missionary protection that professing faith in Christianity brought him.[9] A case in point is how Ukpabio and other slaves stood up to King Eyo Honesty II on the basis of their "faith," refusing to work on the Sabbath, without incurring the certain execution that would have been guaranteed in pre-missionary times. Dickie attributes this to boldness born of faith in Christ. But it is not difficult to see that Ukpabio's status as the first convert to be baptized in Calabar after many years of ministry would have brought upon the court of King Eyo the wrath of the Europeans had he been executed according to Ekpe law. Not surprisingly, the first converts were those who had much to gain from the protection of the Mission House, to the chagrin of the ruling classes: "In the year 1854 no fewer than thirteen young men and two young women were admitted into the fellowship of the Church."[10]

The emergence of boarding schools as a part of the Mission House meant that missionaries had more time and opportunity to shape their wards into future teachers, pastors and leaders according to missionary ideals of Christianity and civility.[11] "The schools had the common aim of propagating the ideals of Christianity and some of the basic doctrines of the particular denomination, while teaching literacy and a little arithmetic to the children."[12]

With respect to the language of instruction, English, the language of commerce and civilization and the road to success and advancement, prevailed.[13] The cultivation of Efik was, therefore, only as the principal means of communicating "oral instruction to the hundreds of thousands, perhaps even

---

8. Knight, "The History of the National Bible Society of Scotland," 161.
9. Dickie, *Story of the Mission in Old Calabar*, 48–49.
10. Dickie, *Story of the Mission in Old Calabar*, 49–50.
11. Ajayi notes that this hope was often realized. "The boarders were in fact personal wards of the missionaries. How many each kept depended on his ability to organize private funds, as the missionary societies did not themselves allocate funds for this purpose." *Christian Missions in Nigeria*, 136–37.
12. Ajayi, *Christian Missions in Nigeria*, 138.
13. Ajayi, *Christian Missions in Nigeria*, 139–40. This was the overwhelming opinion of the Calabarese themselves and of many, though not all, European missionaries.

millions ... who may never be able to acquire a knowledge of English."[14] The vernacular was, therefore, fundamentally the language of religious instruction:

> Although English generally remained the language of instruction, by the 1850s many missionaries were insisting that Religious Knowledge should be taught mainly, if not solely, in the vernacular, which the children most readily comprehended. Thus while ... subjects like Grammar, Spelling and the Meaning of Words undoubtedly referred to the English language, and nobody thought of writing textbooks in the vernacular for subjects like Arithmetic or Geography, as soon as they were available the vernacular Bible and Catechism tended to supplant the English original.[15]

It is in this sense that vernacular Bible translations became an integral part of the educational process. It is also in the same sense that the emerging generation of the Calabarese, while not necessarily Christian, were influenced away from their Calabarese customs through an encounter with Indo-European expositions of Christianity, even though the Bible and Catechism were Efik translations.

We have already encountered those who argue that reading the Bible for themselves in the vernacular was, for the natives, a subversive experience because it presented them with the opportunity to engage directly with the message of the Bible. But even this subversion was in spite of, not because of, the way the Bible was approached and taught by the missionaries and would only become a significant revolutionary force outside the reach of European hegemony. This was still several years away in the Calabar of the 1860s. Further, as I have argued elsewhere, it was a subversion that did not keep pace with the overt westernization of African consciousness, particularly in the subsequent generations of Africans. As Mbiti observes:

> In addition [to indigenous African languages] there are European languages – English, French, Portuguese, Afrikaans and Spanish – being spoken with local modifications, mainly in areas of former colonial rule. French and English are the main international languages; they are here to stay, and we might as well consider them as "African" languages, since they are the greatest legacy we have inherited from colonial powers, and this inheritance nobody can take away from us ... [In addition,] one gets the

---

14. Waddell, "Report of Creek Town Mission for 1854," cited by Ajayi in *Christian Missions in Nigeria*, 140.

15. Ajayi, *Christian Missions in Nigeria*, 140.

impression that the majority of African youth are more interested in learning and mastering a Euro-African language like English or French, than in spending their energies on national tribal languages. Whatever feelings and arguments one might privately have concerning the language problem in Africa, we must face facts and reality. Some of the traditional languages are dying out, partly because the peoples who spoke them may be dying out, but chiefly because of modern type of education and the drift of the population from rural to urban areas.[16]

The mission school, then, was associated with

drawing away children physically into the mission village or at least mentally and spiritually away from the family compounds. One result of this was that, inevitably, the children tended to regard themselves as better than their mates and elders, who did not belong to the new life of the Mission House.[17]

For example, these were the origins of a new Elite in Nigeria, an elite that was to increasingly gravitate towards Indo-European values, rationality and practice.[18]

In the light of the above, we may safely surmise that the chief impact of the Efik New Testament was its contribution to the development of the mindset of the new elite in Calabar. And, in keeping with Duff's agenda in Calcutta,[19] this was a mindset that gravitated towards Western rationality and Christianity according to Scottish Presbyterianism.

Edward Blyden, born in the Dutch West Indies and brought up in the Presbyterian Church, was ahead of his time in recognizing the epistemological hegemony or "mental subservience to others" that Christianity was cast in. He personally turned to Islam "not because he was converted to it but, as he later explained, because it was more 'African,' and he considered it would be better for the African to pass gradually through Islam to Christianity."[20]

---

16. Mbiti, *African Religions & Philosophy*, 101. See also Nyirenda, "Epistemological Hegemony in the History of Christianity in Africa."

17. Ajayi, *Christian Missions in Nigeria*, 142–43; Grimley and Robinson, *Church Growth in Central and Southern Nigeria*, 276.

18. "The emigrants and converts were in fact trying to become what the missionaries hoped they would, a rich, inventive, powerful middle-class . . . They were loud in their profession of their faith and generally supporters of missionary work. They owned 'pawns' and domestic slaves, usually under the guise of redeeming them, but . . . many missionaries did the same." Ajayi, *Christian Missions in Nigeria*, 165.

19. See Maxwell on Alexander Duff's educational policy in Calcutta above.

20. Ajayi, *Christian Missions in Nigeria*, 266.

Part III

The ChiChewa Bible Translation Project

Part III

8

Background to the Livingstonia and Blantyre Missions

Since the ChiChewa Bible translation project spans generally the same time period as the Efik New Testament project, and since it is also a product of Scottish Presbyterianism, there is a lot of overlap between the two projects.

Robert Laws went to Central Africa under the auspices of the Free Church of Scotland Foreign Missions Committee (FMC), the denomination behind Livingstonia Mission, although he was an ordained minister of the United Presbyterian Church.[1] This duality came to an end in October 1900 when the Free Church of Scotland and the United Presbyterian Church merged to form the United Free Church.[2] Henry Henderson came to Central Africa in the company of the Laws party to find a suitable place for the establishment of a second mission under the auspices of the Established Church of Scotland.[3]

These differences meant very little as far as the missions were concerned. For example, it was the venerable Alexander Duff, a Church of Scotland minister now turned missionary statesman and Dr. Goold, representing the Reformed Presbyterian Church, who sent off Robert Laws.[4] While in Central Africa, Young and Laws were the *de facto* heads of both mission stations until the Established Church of Scotland sent reinforcements for the Blantyre Mission.[5] Given this history, and in the interest of space, we will only highlight those aspects that are distinctive to Central Africa.

---

1. McIntosh, *Robert Laws*, 9–13, 16–19, 26.

2. McIntosh, *Robert Laws*, 144.

3. Ross, *Blantyre Mission*, 16, 22; W. P. Livingstone, *Laws of Livingstonia* (London: Hodder & Stoughton, 1921), 41, 42.

4. McIntosh, *Robert Laws*, 23–24.

5. Pages 49–50. See NLS 7876/151, Mins. of Meeting at Blantyre.

Nida notes that: "A 'Union' version of ChiNyanja has been described as a literary language for use by speakers of all the Nyanja dialects. It has come into use for education, administration, and in the development of vernacular literature."[6] Binnington's account is more revealing:

> At the beginning of this century, work was started on a new version to embrace the Southern and Western dialects: first a tentative Gospel was produced (1901), then the New Testament (1906), the Psalms (1911) and finally the "Union" Bible (1922). The 1936 revision of the latter is the Bible in use to the present day among the large numbers of Nyanja-speaking Protestants.[7]

Since the translation work of the Universities Mission to Central Africa (UMCA) – a mission of the Anglican Church based at Likoma – was not a part of the Union Nyanja project, it will not be included in our analysis.[8]

However, because the Union Nyanja Bible was a revision of work compiled from the translation work of different translators and in the various dialects, we will, to appreciate the process focus on the work of two major contributors: Laws of Livingstonia Mission and Scott of Blantyre Mission. We will focus on their approach to their translation work in the light of their privileged status as European missionaries. In addition, here, we will conduct a basic analysis of a translated segment of the biblical texts. The text for our analysis will be Laws' because of its direct geographic and ethnic identification with the Chewa, and the availability of his original drafts in the archives of the Bible Society of Scotland, Edinburgh.

Nyanja, a term that literally means "lake" or "expanse of water" of which "nyassa" or "nyasa" is a variant, is also the noun for the people of the area – the Nyanja or the Mang'anja – and the language group to which several dialects in the area belong. "Livingstone had first set eyes on the lake on 16th September 1859 – and gave it the name Lake Nyasa . . . It looks as if the explorer misunderstood the word and took it to be the actual name of the lake."[9]

ChiChewa, with the prefix *Chi-* standing as a pointer to the impersonal nature of the noun following, is one such dialect. Its speakers are accordingly called A-Chewa, where the prefix *A-* points to both the personal nature

---

6. Nida, *Book of a Thousand Tongues*, 336.

7. J. D. Binnington, "Where Have All The Bibles Gone?" Internal note (Edinburgh: Scottish Bible Society, 1986).

8. Nida, *Book of a Thousand Tongues*, 335; Coldham, *African Scriptures*, vol. II, 512–27; Ross, *Blantyre Mission*, 180.

9. McIntosh, *Robert Laws*, 37.

and plurality of the noun following, or simply Chewa. Within the larger classification of *Nyanja*, Chewa is known as Western Nyanja. "The numerous ChiNyanja dialects are greatly variant, the Eastern form showing particular divergence."[10]

In the words of D. C. Scott, "the Mang'anja form part of the great River and Lake branch of the Bantu race, and Chimang'anja is the language of the River or Lake (*Nyasa, nyanja, ng'anja, nyanza* meaning lake, river, or water). The dialects of *Chikunda, Ambo, Chipeta, Anguru*, are slightly modified Mang'anja."[11]

According to B. Pachai,

> what started off as Maravi ended as Chewa, Mang'anja, Nyanja, Chipeta, Nsenga, Chikunda, Ntumba, and Zimba. This came about as a result of dispersion and decentralisation, and the various names are no more than regional or geographical designations of people who belonged to the same cultural and language group. Of these, the name Chewa stands out as the numerically strongest group, of whom about 80 per cent live in Malawi and the remaining 20 per cent or so in Zambia and Mozambique.[12]

Since political independence in 1964, Malawi has, for political reasons, adopted the term "ChiChewa" for what in reality is Union Nyanja, a literary language created by combining Western and Southern Nyanja. "ChiNyanja," however, remains the term used in neighbouring Zambia.[13]

The Historical Forces behind Livingstonia and Blantyre Missions

Scottish missions to Central Africa were a direct consequence of the legacy of David Livingstone, himself a Scot.[14] Livingstone's journeys had been inspired by his vision to see, through Christianity and commerce, Africa become an

---

10. Nida, *Book of a Thousand Tongues*, 335.
11. Scott, *A Cyclopaedic Dictionary of the Mang'anja*, v.
12. B. Pachai, *Malawi: The History of the Nation* (London: Longman, 1973), 6.
13. Binnington, "Where Have All The Bibles Gone?"
14. Livingstone first visited the area in 1859 and recommended it because of its favourable climate and topography, for European settlement and development as a base to combat slave trade and preach the gospel. Ross, *Blantyre Mission*, 14–15. On 26 May 1874, in a speech by Dr. James Stewart of Lovedale Mission, South Africa, to the General Assembly of the Free Church in Edinburgh, he urged the desirability of "setting up in Central Africa a mission station to be known as LIVINGSTONIA in memory of David Livingstone." McIntosh, *Robert Laws*, 13; J. Stewart, *Livingstonia: its Origins* (Edinburgh: Andrew Elliot, 1894), 47; A. Hetherwick, *The Romance of Blantyre: How Livingstone's Dream Came True* (London: Clarke & Company, Ltd., 1931), 13.

economic player in the world and its people on the road to Christianity and civilization.[15] However, he was part of a larger dynamic at home:

> Scotland had an Enlightenment tradition which encouraged scientific research . . . The geographical exploration associated with nineteenth-century mission work was in accordance with such a tradition. A further factor is the Calvinist work ethic in Scottish Presbyterianism, which was to be brought to Africa in accordance with Livingstone's call for "legitimate commerce and Christianity."[16]

The Central Africa of the 1850s was a relative haven of peace in spite of the presence of a culture of commercial slave trade.[17] Yao emigration from northern Mozambique into the Shire highlands had spelled the first intrusion into this haven.[18] But this was nothing compared to the destabilization brought about by the rampaging Ngoni, "propelled northwards from Natal by the exploits of Shaka."[19]

In this vortex, the coming of Scottish missionaries, with the promise of European economic and military advantage that they represented, was a challenge to Ngoni hegemony.[20] This was particularly the case with respect to Livingstonia Mission at its Bandawe headquarters where the location of mission stations became a matter of political diplomacy because of the implications it had for the balance of power in the area. In the words of Thompson, for the Ngoni,

> There were two main factors at work in any relationship which might develop with the newcomers. The first was the possibility

---

15. Ross, *Blantyre Mission*, 63.

16. P. G. Forster, "Missionaries and Anthropology: The Case of the Scots of Northern Malawi," *Journal of Religion in Africa* XVI, 2 (1986): 103.

17. Ross, *Blantyre Mission*, 14; McIntosh, *Robert Laws*, 46. In the words of Dr. Stewart, Arab slave traders were Central Africa's worst enemy. Proceedings RGS Vol.1, 1879, 303. The history of the Maravi migration, Bantu-speaking people of whom the thirteenth- to sixteenth-century AD settlers in most of central and southern Malawi were a part, need not concern us here. For an account of this migration see Pachai, *Malawi*, 4–9.

18. Ross, *Blantyre Mission*, 15. Cf. K. M. Phiri, "Yao Intrusion into Southern Malawi, Nyanja Resistance, and Colonial Conquest, 1830–1900," *Transafrican Journal of History* 13 (1984): 157–76.

19. I. Linden, "The Maseko Ngoni at Domwe, 1870–1900," in *Early History of Malawi*, edited by B. Pachai (London: Longmans, 1972), 237–51. Also see Pachai, *Malawi*, 22–24.

20. It was, apparently, the "military strength and formidable social organisation of the Ngoni" that made them a dominant force, subduing "most of the autochthonous people in the vicinity." Ross, *Blantyre Mission*, 15–16. Also see Pachai, *Malawi*, 25.

of a military (or at any rate a political) alliance which could enable them better to confront their enemies on the lakeshore; the second, which developed gradually over the next few years, was the tactic of using the missionaries as alternative religious practitioners who might have the spiritual power to bring rain, or to ensure successful crops[21]

The policy of the Free Church FMC on slavery under which Laws went to Central Africa was that elimination of the trade in the long term was more important than achieving the immediate release of any particular group of captives.[22] He came to Central Africa when the local Mang'anja were not masters of their own fate.[23] Arabs trading through the East Coast of Africa masterminded the slave trade of the time:

> Mr Young reported one slaver's estimate that some 10,000 slaves were carried across Lake Nyasa from west to east each year on their way to the east coast. These figures have been challenged, but Roland Oliver has shown that the custom-house records, at the single port of Kilwa alone, record as many as 22,000 slaves in 1866; he estimates that more than three times that number reached the coast every year from some part of the interior.[24]

Livingstonia Mission was entered with a clear intent to evangelize and, particularly, civilize as a means towards realizing Livingstone's vision:

> While recognising that the proclamation of the Gospel would be central to its message ... those who supported the mission were aiming from the start at a mission which should be "Evangelistic, Educational, and Industrial." As well as preaching the Gospel, the Mission would aim at training the young at least to read and write, and would also give training in practical skills, helping to introduce the arts of civilised life and so develop that legitimate

---

21. Thompson, *Touching the Heart*, 71, 81.

22. McIntosh, *Robert Laws*, 26.

23. He came "at a time when it could take ten months to receive a reply to letters home. He went out when the true source of Malaria was unidentified, and when the debilitating effects of fever were almost unavoidable. He found thousands living behind stockades, or high up on mountain ledges, some in fear of the fierce Angoni warriors ... and some in fear of slave traders." McIntosh, *Robert Laws*, 2.

24. McIntosh, *Robert Laws*, 25. See also E. D. Young, *Mission to Nyassa, a Journal of Adventures* (London, 1877), 54, 77, 99–108, 193; Oliver, *Missionary Factor in East Africa*, 15 note 3.

trade of which Livingstone often spoke as one of the most powerful means of repressing the abominable traffic in human flesh and blood.[25]

Generally, Central Africans did not have the same pre-missionary era appreciation for trade-related education that we found in West Africa. But this did not stop them from cooperating with the missionaries' educational programs. A case in point is the progress at Cape Maclear, the first location of Livingstonia Mission. Building on the legacy of Livingstone in the area, the initial party declared their interests to Chief M'ponda, who was the overlord of the land around Cape Maclear, asking for permission to settle in the vicinity.[26] In their request they indicated their intention to teach his people about God and the arts of civilization: "When they asked for land on which to settle M'ponda told them to choose for themselves."[27]

This is comparable to the speed and generosity with which land was allocated to Waddell's party in Duke Town, Old Calabar. When they made contact with Chief Makanjira in the east side of the Lake, "he did not object to a doctor or a teacher coming to live in his village, or to his people supplying the mission party with food. Meantime, another chief, Chimlolo, had been talking of settling beside the mission."[28]

The beginnings of education work in Central Africa were without trumpets but just as enduring:

> One of the boys who had been taught the alphabet one day returned a few weeks later with some friends bringing with them "batata" or "sweet potatoes" for sale. Laws was pleased to find that the boy remembered a good deal of what he had been taught, and a class of boys anxious to learn the alphabet now began. This may be regarded as the beginning of educational work at Livingstonia.[29]

---

25. McIntosh, *Robert Laws*, 27; *East Central Africa, Livingstonia: The Mission to Lake Nyassa*, 2nd ed. (Edinburgh: Free Church, 1876), 12. Thompson demonstrates the centrality of education in the Scottish understanding of civilizing through the example of Lovedale Mission: "From the beginning of their work the Scots stressed the importance of education as part of the social and cultural transformation which they understood to be a part of their mission." *Touching the Heart*, 9.

26. NLS 7907, Laws' Diary, 11/10/1875.

27. NLS 7907, Laws' Diary, 11/10/1875.

28. McIntosh, *Robert Laws*, 39.

29. NLS 7907, Laws' Diary, 19/5/1876, 12/6/1876; McIntosh, *Robert Laws*, 40.

In his 1878 report to Scotland, Laws indicated, among other things, progress in three areas. Under "Educational," he noted that

> The school roll had risen over the past year from 29 boys to 65. The latter figure must have included girls, since girls are mentioned as being among the prize-winners in August. The day began with a half hour Bible lesson. Writing and Arithmetic, including multiplication in the advanced classes, was taught. In addition, two hours a day were spent on manual labour, chiefly work in the fields or in cleaning the roads and grounds of the station.[30]

Generally, the same social-cultural practices encountered in Old Calabar were obtaining here. There was the custom of trying to establish the guilt or innocence of a person accused of witchcraft or some other crime by forcing them to drink the *mwavi* (poison) though, this time, it was made from the bark of a tree, not powdered esere-bean.[31] This is, of course, a feature of the widespread belief in African cosmology that God, as ultimate judge, should not or cannot be approached directly, but through the mediation of other persons or beings.[32] In this understanding, the ordeal is not an arbitrary barbaric act but is the verdict of the highest court available to mankind. Laws had grasped the import of *mwavi* when he likened it to "an omniscient God, able to kill the guilty and to spare the innocent."[33]

The birth of twins was a bad omen and, in this case, apparently required the death of the mother.[34] The mission compound soon became, as in Calabar, a sanctuary for runaway slaves and others ostracized and condemned by society. Before too long, the mission compound had evolved into an alternative principality to those of tribal chiefs.[35]

---

30. NLS 7876/244, R. Laws, Report for 1878.
31. McIntosh, *Robert Laws*, 40. See also Dickie, *Story of the Mission in Old Calabar*, 44.
32. Mbiti, *African Religions & Philosophy*, 68–71.
33. NLS 7907, Laws' Diary, 28/5/1876.
34. McIntosh, *Robert Laws*, 41. Cf. NLS 7907, Laws' Diary, 1/6/1876, 31/5/1876, where Laws gives an account of a woman who fled to the mission compound to escape death for giving birth to twins.
35. McIntosh, *Robert Laws*, 41, 58–62. "By the summer of 1879 there were some 360 Africans resident around the station at Cape Maclear, with 1000 at Kaning'ina and the Glasgow Committee resolved to ask the Government to establish consular authority over the area." NLS 7912, Mins. of Liv. Sub-Com. 6/6/1879.

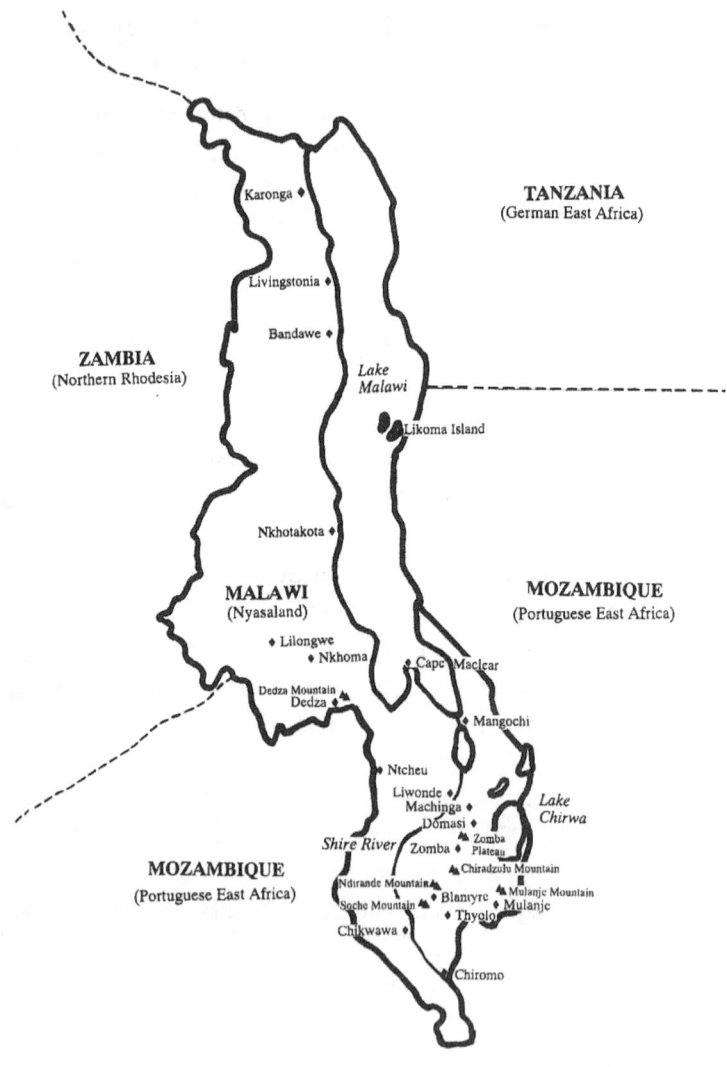

Figure 3. Map of modern Malawi showing Blantyre and the successive headquarters of Livingstonia Mission: Cape Maclear, Bandawe and Livingstonia.[36]

---

36. A. C. Ross, *Blantyre Mission and the Making of Modern Malawi* (Blantyre, Malawi: CLAIM), 1996, 197. Used with permission.

9

Origins and History: Livingstonia and Blantyre Missions

Livingstonia and Blantyre Missions entered Central Africa at the same time: Both missions had been suggested in the aftermath of Livingstone's funeral but whereas [missionaries of] the Free Church Livingstonia mission were recruited and on their way to Africa less than a year after the original appeal by James Stewart in May 1874, the Church of Scotland mission had, in the same period, managed to gather only one recruit. This was Henry Henderson – a Scot of wide practical experiences, including a period as a sheep farmer in Australia. In the absence of any colleagues the Foreign Mission Committee Blantyre subcommittee agreed to send him out with the pioneer Livingstonia party in 1875. His task was to look for a suitable site while further missionaries were recruited.[1]

Livingstonia Mission

The inspirational nature of Livingstone's journeys for his mission does not need further elaboration. Following Dr. Stewart's urging at the General Assembly of 1874, a resolution was passed to found the Livingstonia Mission as an industrial and educational settlement.[2]

---

1. Thompson, *Touching the Heart*, 58.
2. This meeting was held in the Queen's Hotel, Glasgow, on 3 November 1874. McIntosh, *Robert Laws*, 113.

The process of raising finances and recruiting personnel that followed yielded bountifully.[3] Robert Laws, as an ordained minister[4] and doctor of medicine, was the only ordained member of the mission party destined for Central Africa. The rest included E. D. Young, an officer of the Royal Navy with experience of sailing on the Zambezi and Shire rivers of Central Africa. He was the leader of the party in place of Dr. James Stewart who was supposed to take over as leader after Young's two years were up. Others were William Baker, an Englishman and navy man; George Johnson, a Scot from Aberdeen and a carpenter; John McFadyen, a Scot from Govan and an engineer and blacksmith; Alan Simpson, a Scot from Cupar, Fife, and an engineer; and Alexander Riddel, a Scot from Leochel-Cushnie, near Alford, on Donside, and an agriculturalist. The presence of Henry Henderson of the Established Church of Scotland has already been mentioned. Laws was appointed second in command and Medical Officer.[5]

Laws' licensing and ordination were combined, contrary to normal practice, presumably to enable him to sail for Africa as an ordained minister.[6] Even his medical credentials were conferred on him contrary to normal practice:

> In the weeks prior to his ordination, Laws had been busy, not only with the subjects on which he was to be examined by the presbytery, but with Practical and Clinical Medicine . . . He passed his exams and graduated MB CH. A Bachelor of Medicine was entitled to graduate "Doctor of Medicine" on attaining the age of twenty-four, provided that he was already Master of Arts, and had, since graduating in Medicine, spent two years in Medical or

---

3. "initial target of £10,000 had been surpassed by £474. £5,587 had been raised by subscriptions in Glasgow and the West of Scotland, £3,705 in Edinburgh, £547 in Aberdeen and £640 in Dundee. On all the Auxiliary Committees the number of lay people greatly exceeded the number of ministers." *Eastern Central Africa*, 44.

4. The recruitment of Laws to this mission was special for several reasons. Loaning him to the Free Church, initially for two years, was viewed by the United Presbyterian Church as a step towards linking the Foreign Mission Committees of the two denominations while the latter decided on its own mission in Central Africa. McIntosh, *Robert Laws*, 16–17.

5. McIntosh, *Robert Laws*, 21–22.

6. SRO CH3/2/14 Aberdeen Presbytery of UPC, Mins. 23/3/1875. Cited in McIntosh, *Robert Laws*, 18. The ethos of the ordination, on the eve of the mission, paralleled that in Goshen in the shadow of the mission to Calabar. "Speaking of the reason for their gathering together that evening, the Moderator said, 'The peculiarity of the case was the charm of it,' referring to the fact that a UP missionary was going out with a Free Church Mission. The mission was to be a 'memorial to our great countryman David Livingstone . . . the grand object . . . the introduction of the Gospel into the dark regions of Central Africa.'" McIntosh, *Robert Laws*, 18. See also Dickie, *Story of the Mission in Old Calabar*, 10–11.

Surgical Practice. Laws' post-graduate experience was not gained through attachment to a hospital, but Aberdeen University wisely accepted that in Central Africa his medical and surgical experience would be of a kind to entitle him to the higher degree, and he became an MD two years after first graduating in medicine.[7]

In the class divisions of the day, this meant that Laws, as doctor and ordained minister, had a higher standing than his colleagues. According to Thompson,

> Even amongst the Scottish missionaries there was a major social division between the ordained and medical men on the one hand and the artisans on the other. This division, which reflected class divisions in British society of the time, could be seen in several ways. The two most obvious perhaps were the difference in salary and in levels of education. While the ordained men had gone right through the educational system to university level, some of the artisans would have left school at twelve or fourteen years of age. Whereas an ordained medical missionary could hope to earn as much as £300 per year, an artisan might expect less than £100.[8]

This was despite being second in command.[9] It is very significant, therefore, that Xhosa evangelists, most of whom were better educated than the Scottish artisans, were initially paid approximately half of the salary of a Scottish artisan. Thompson suggests that this was the case because of racial differentials in South Africa where their wage was the equivalent of a Black ordained minister in the Eastern Cape. But the observation is important to note because it sheds some light on the sort of recognition that the intellectual contribution of a Xhosa member of the party, let alone a Mang'anja, would carry in an activity as esoteric as strict Bible interpretation and linguistic study.[10]

Thompson has also pointed out that, given the attitudes and practices of the times, minimal mention or even omission did not always mean lack of involvement. For instance, he observes

---

7. McIntosh, *Robert Laws*, 19.

8. Thompson, *Touching the Heart*, 38.

9. Indeed, pragmatic accounts like Forster's portray him as the central figure. "The beginnings of missionary penetration into the north of Malawi were in 1877 when Robert Laws, an ordained minister also qualified as a medical doctor, set out with artisans to establish a station." "Missionaries and Anthropology," 105–106. Yet Young was the first to circumnavigate Lake Nyasa. Proceedings of RGS Vol. 1 1879, 289ff; McIntosh, *Robert Laws*, 45.

10. Thompson, *Touching the Heart*, 38–39.

That Koyi established his general usefulness during the second circum-navigation in 1878 cannot be gauged by public references to him in writing about the journey, for, to take one example, when Stewart read a paper describing the journey to the Royal Geographical Society on 10 March 1879, only one mention was made of Koyi in the entire lecture. Detailed references to the contributions of Africans in such situations were extremely rare. Rather, we can assume his usefulness from the fact that he became an almost permanent fixture on such journeys in the next few years.[11]

Nevertheless, it is highly unlikely that even Koyi's implicit usefulness extended to making critical choices in the reduction of the Mang'anja dialects, languages that were as foreign to him as they were to the Europeans, into writing. Koyi's linguistic and cultural advantage was only in relation to the Nguni language of the Ngoni that was related to his own Xhosa.[12]

Cape Maclear on the shores of the Lake was the first location of Livingstonia Mission. From the start, Laws applied himself to learning Mang'anja. Riddel also engaged in linguistic studies and even published a dictionary and grammar of Chinyanja ahead of Laws.[13] From Cape Maclear, Young and Laws explored the length of the lake.

In keeping with the paternalistic tendency by European explorers to mark their "discoveries" by naming geographical landmarks that already had local names, Young "named the steep range of mountains on the east side of it at its northern end 'The Livingstone Mountains,' and gave Horace Waller's name to the steep peak on the west side near which the Livingstonia Institution was to be built many years later."[14] On a subsequent exploratory journey, Stewart and Laws named a bay on the west side of Lake Nyassa "Florence Bay" after Stewart's daughter.[15]

Dr. Stewart had arrived from Lovedale on 21 October 1876 to take charge of Livingstonia when Captain Young left for home. But this was a short-lived

---

11. Thompson, *Touching the Heart*, 46.

12. Thompson, *Touching the Heart*, 47–48.

13. "When Riddel returned to Scotland in 1879 the Glasgow Committee agreed to publish 200 copies of a Dictionary and Grammar of the Chinyanja language prepared by him. In the event, 500 copies were printed and a gift of 15 guineas was made to Riddel in recognition of his work." McIntosh, *Robert Laws*, 36.

14. Young, *Mission to Nyassa*, 111, 119.

15. McIntosh, *Robert Laws*, 46.

charge as he was now head of Lovedale (in modern day South Africa) where his wife was in residence.¹⁶ After Stewart, Laws was the inevitable choice for leader.¹⁷ In his note to Duff, Stewart hinted at Laws' impending role as leader:

> I sincerely hope that all idea has been given up of recalling Dr. Laws merely because his period of engagement is nearly expired. . . . If the Committee is really desirous that the Livingstonia Mission succeed, *they will retain Dr. Laws till* he himself wishes to go – which he does not at present.¹⁸

Cape Maclear proved to be unsuitable for several reasons. The soil near the station was unsuitable for the production of ordinary crops. The area lacked water for irrigation in addition to being small and restrictive. Tsetse fly was prevalent.¹⁹

Subsequent exploratory journeys in autumn 1877, August 1878 and November 1878 ensued in a "better site" for the mission. Because this was Ngoni territory, William Koyi became a permanent feature of these explorations because of his ability to converse directly with the Ngoni.²⁰ Initially built as an observation post, Bandawe became the new headquarters of Livingstonia Mission on 27 October 1881. Meanwhile, Laws' and Koyi's explorations further north led to the establishment of a station at Kaning'ina.²¹ These were to prove to be the foundations of missionary work among both the Atonga and Angoni.²² Another significant development during this period was the founding of the Livingstonia Central Africa Company, incorporated in June 1878:

> Later, it was known as the African Lakes Corporation and as the African Lakes Company. Its purpose was to "encourage legitimate and beneficial trade amongst the natives," to "promote civilizations" and "to assist to a great extent in the suppression of the slave trade." It was thus following the lines recommended by David Livingstone to replace the slave trade with legitimate commerce, but from the

---

16. McIntosh, *Robert Laws*, 42–43. See also B. Pachai, ed., *Livingstone, Man of Africa, Memorial Essays 1873–1973* (London, 1973), 224.

17. "It was becoming increasingly clear that when he left the mantle of leadership was likely to fall on the shoulders of Robert Laws. He was still in his mid-twenties, but both E. D. Young and Dr. James Stewart spoke of him in the highest terms." Young, *Mission to Nyassa*, 86.

18. NLS 7876, Jas. Stewart to Dr. Duff, from Blantyre, 20/12/1876.

19. McIntosh, *Robert Laws*, 44.

20. McIntosh, *Robert Laws*, 45, 50, 52.

21. McIntosh, *Robert Laws*, 52, 74.

22. NLS 7909, Cape Maclear Scroll Mins. 13/12/1878.

beginning there were interior arrangements with the Livingstonia and Blantyre missions to manage the purchase of their supplies.²³

Laws became the leader of Livingstonia Mission in November 1877 when Stewart returned to Lovedale.²⁴ Koyi's profile grew immensely. His multifaceted profile is perhaps best encapsulated in the reactions to his death. To the Scots, he was a testament to the potential for the civilization of Africans: "Without any doubt Koyi's Scottish colleagues thought very highly of him, but they did so for a rather contorted reason – because they saw him as approximating their own Eurocentric ideas of a civilized Christian gentleman."²⁵ To the Ngoni, he was *umteteleli*, as "the one for speaking between us" – that is, between the Ngoni and the missionaries. In other words, he was one who could identify and empathize with them while at the same time being a part of the missionary contingent.²⁶

However, the activities of the African Lakes Company notwithstanding, there were no obvious commercial interests in the areas surrounding Livingstonia and Blantyre Missions. Therefore, it took stronger lobbying²⁷ to convince the British Government to establish a Protectorate than was necessary in Calabar where the combined presence of British supercargoes and the British Navy preceded the mission to Old Calabar.²⁸ Part of the pressure that led to a Protectorate was generated by the skirmishes that agents of the African Lakes Company began to have with Arab slave traders and the sentiment among the African Lakes Company that the British Government was not giving as much support as it should. This, coupled with the pressure of the Livingstonia Sub-Committee along with representatives of the Established Church of Scotland, led to changes in the Government's dealings with Central Africa.²⁹

---

23. NLS 8021, Livingstonia Central Africa Co. Prospectus, 1878.

24. J. Wells, *Stewart of Lovedale* (London: Hodder & Stoughton, 1908), 141.

25. Thompson, *Touching the Heart*, 132; "In Memorium William Koyi," *Christian Express* (Sept. 1886), 1.

26. Thompson, *Touching the Heart*, 118.

27. McIntosh records how Consul O'Neill, based in Mozambique, told Laws that the mission had no right to receive fugitive slaves. Upon appeal to the Foreign Office in England, Lord Granville's response was that "the only rights enjoyed by the Mission are those conceded by local chiefs." NLS 7912, 28/6/1881, containing Lord Granville's letter of 11/5/1881.

28. Because of this, Mission in Central Africa "was to be found among the strongest advocates of the establishment of a Protectorate by the British Government, a step not taken until 1891 and taken then with great reluctance." McIntosh, *Robert Laws*, 64, 101ff.

29. McIntosh, *Robert Laws*, 101ff. It may be argued, therefore, that the safety of British citizens was a larger incentive for the British Government's presence in Central Africa than any other factor.

Blantyre Mission

Although Blantyre Mission shares the same foundation with Livingstonia Mission, its specific evolution was different. According to Ross, following the funeral of Livingstone in 1874, a wave of enthusiasm in Scotland was followed by years during which concern was maintained at a high level. This

> Golden era of Scottish Missionary activity extended to 1914, the onset of the First World War. With respect to Blantyre Mission, this era may be divided into three parts: 1874–1881, when Macrae of Hawick first suggested the setting up of the mission until its reconstitution by David Clement Scott; 1881–1898, the era of Scott's leadership; and 1898–1914, a period when Alexander Hetherwick was at the helm.[30]

Unlike Livingstonia Mission, however, Blantyre Mission did not attract adequate finances or personnel.[31] When reinforcements for Henderson arrived in the summer of 1876, none of them was ordained. Six recruits were in this party: T. Thornton Macklin, a doctor; and five artisans – John Buchanan, Jonathan Duncan, George Fenwick, William Milne, and John Walker.[32] They turned out to be an addition to his problems rather than a solution. Macklin and his party arrived at Blantyre in a state of near collapse both physically and psychologically; and coming to a derelict station did not help.[33]

Further, the spiritual credentials of most of them were suspect. As Thompson notes, the personalities and characters of the new party were the largest drawback.

> So desperate for recruits were the Blantyre subcommittee that they had accepted several volunteers who were little more than adventurers . . . both Macklin and Buchanan were men of Christian conviction; Duncan was later to do some good work as a gardener and agriculturalist; but the others, especially Walker and Fenwick were very rough diamonds indeed. Two months later, no

---

30. *Blantyre Mission*, 17. Also see Hetherwick, *The Romance of Blantyre*, 13ff.
31. There was never a time when Blantyre Mission was financially worry-free. In fact, overspending, to the chagrin of the Convenor of the FMC, was a very common practice for the duration of Scott's tenure. Ross, *Blantyre Mission*, 24.
32. Ross, *Blantyre Mission*, 19.
33. D. Macdonald, *Africana: or the Heart of Heathen Africa*, vol. 2 (Edinburgh: John Menzies, 1882), 21.

real progress of any kind had been made and Henderson (who in any case had hoped to be on his way home by now) was in despair.[34]

Blantyre Mission dates its origins to the arrival of this eclectic party in October 1876.[35] Shortly afterwards, Henderson sought the help of Laws at Cape Maclear.[36] A visit by Drs Stewart and Laws in response to Henderson's summons led to a decision that, in the interest of mission, Dr. Stewart should take charge for a while:

> After that Dr. Laws would serve for some months followed by Dr. Black with William Koyi the Xhosa evangelist, as teacher, and Thomas Boquito as manual worker and interpreter. The Established Church of Scotland would pay the salaries of the men from the Free Church Mission for the period they served at Blantyre.[37]

The supervision of the Livingstonia missionaries, particularly that of James Stewart CE, a cousin to Dr. James Stewart, kept the mission afloat until Dr. Macklin had gained enough confidence to take over leadership. James Stewart CE arrived at Cape Maclear on 24 February 1877. He relocated to Blantyre on 10 April 1877 and for most of the next eighteen months was the *de facto* head of the Blantyre Mission:

> His engineering skills and his general enthusiasm kick-started the mission by beginning with a series of basic and essential physical tasks for which he was professionally well-qualified . . . Mapasa Ntintili and William Koyi did much to supplement it in terms of providing basic mission work in the areas of education and evangelism.[38]

---

34. Thompson, *Touching the Heart*, 60; Ross, *Blantyre Mission*, 20.

35. Thompson, *Touching the Heart*, 59.

36. "Dr Macklin, because of his health, felt he could not undertake some of the work needing to be done, while some of the artisans, who had come out with the second party were discontented partly because they were not doing what they considered their own proper work." McIntosh, *Robert Laws*, 49.

37. NLS 7876/151, Mins. of meeting at Blantyre, cited in McIntosh, *Robert Laws*, 50.

38. Thompson, *Touching the Heart*, 62–67; J. Thompson, ed., *From Nyassa to Tanganyika: The Journal of James Stewart CE in Central Africa 1876–1879* (Blantyre, Malawi: Central Africana, 1989), 2; A. Ross, "Livingstone and the Aftermath: The Origins & Development of the Blantyre Mission" in Pachai, *Livingstone, Man of Africa*, 199–200; Hetherwick, *The Romance of Blantyre*, 28–28.

Macklin remained in charge until the Rev. Duff MacDonald arrived in July 1878. The delicate matter of the emergence of the mission compound as an alternative principality to native authorities took a more sinister form at Blantyre Mission and led to what is known as the Blantyre Crisis. The tension of judicial liberties, present in Calabar, was also at the Missions in Central Africa. As Thompson notes,

> There can be no doubt that in the very difficult situation in which both missions found themselves in the limbo between traditional African law and colonial control each resorted to physical punishment and imprisonment to deal with offences (or perceived offences) taking place, not only on mission property, but also beyond. If there was a difference between them, it was that the practice was carried out at Livingstonia with somewhat more restraint and control than at Blantyre where, in the absence of strong leadership, it undoubtedly got out of control.[39]

According to Thompson, the absence of precise instructions for the mission at Blantyre may have been responsible for the excesses that led to this crisis.[40] However, the fact that Blantyre Mission was from the very beginning envisaged to be a colony partly made up of freed slaves, may have had a part to play in the overt nature of missionary authority there.[41] Nevertheless, Hetherwick held the missionaries totally responsible:

> No excuse of inexperience or lack of definite instructions could lessen the gravity of the acts committed in these difficult times. All over Central Africa the success or failure of any policy – whether civil, commercial or mission – is a matter of personnel and personality. And Blantyre in its early days suffered in both of these directions.[42]

D. C. Scott came in 1881 with a mission to reconstitute the Mission and to put the crisis behind. The man and his ideas of mission dominated his era. Scott was an enigma. He came intent on bringing the gospel and modern

---

39. Thompson, *Touching the Heart*, 72.
40. Thompson, *Touching the Heart*, 68–70.
41. Ross, *Blantyre Mission*, 31.
42. Hetherwick, *The Romance of Blantyre*, 31.

culture.⁴³ To Scott, an African gained equality in more than spiritual affairs by becoming a member of the Christian church; and the African's assimilation of modern culture was not at the expense of his or her own culture, but entailed a fertilization of African culture by European culture.⁴⁴ Yet his esteem of Africans, their culture(s), and their potential was without equal in Central African Missions. It was his manifest belief that Africans were not only capable, but were ready for responsibility both in the church and in the new society created in Africa by the coming of European power.⁴⁵

His stance is even the more significant because he came to reconstitute the Mission under recommendations that were contrary to his approach. The recommendations arising from the enquiry into the Blantyre Crisis were as follows. The work should be clearly and simply evangelistic in nature. Consequently, staffing recommendations were meant to lead to stoppage of any kind of sophisticated instruction of African people or a concern for their medical care. The rationale was that successful evangelism could take place apart from any great cultural change among African people and that the care of the sick was not an essential part but a subordinate adjunct to the work of evangelism.⁴⁶ The tenor of the Rev. Dr. Thomas Rankine's and Thomas Pringle's recommendations were endorsed by the General Assembly of 1881 and Livingstone's vision of mission as Christianity and responsible commerce was effectively rejected.⁴⁷

However, this enigma is perhaps resolved when we recall that, to Scott, modern culture was not simply European culture but a culture of universal proportions to which the African had as much right as the European.⁴⁸ Partly because of the overwhelming support by most of the personnel at Blantyre

---

43. Ross, *Blantyre Mission*, 63. His theory was that "Africans were part of the same humanity as Scotsmen or Portuguese, that they could contribute to the Christian Church as well as receive from it, that the civilising and Christianising task of the mission must result in a civilisation and Church that was African as well as being Christian" (67). Later on, we will show how this commitment is intricately linked to the phenomenon of epistemologically Westernized Africans that continues to plague the continent to this day.

44. Ross, *Blantyre Mission*, 66.

45. Ross, *Blantyre Mission*, 63. In fact, he understood that participation was an integral part of the Africans' learning process and development of potential. See his article in *Life and Work in British Central Africa*, June 1895, a publication that later assumed the title *Life and Work in Nyasaland* during the period 1888–1919.

46. Assembly Reports, 1881, FMC Report, Appendix A, 86–90.

47. Ross, *Blantyre Mission*, 65. See also Cairns, *Prelude to Imperialism*, 219; MacDonald, *African*, vol. 2, 248.

48. Ross, *Blantyre Mission*, 63.

Mission,⁴⁹ he was able to direct the mission according to his convictions, and not according to the recommendations of the Foreign Missions Committee. In addition, Scott, like Goldie in Calabar, was profoundly aware of the reality that he was a part of the missionary effort of a conquering nation going to the conquered, in contrast with the biblical Paul who was of a poorer and colonized nation going to the expanse of the Roman Empire. Scott recognized this as the most challenging problem of his appointment to Africa.⁵⁰

Scott had trouble with fellow missionaries who typified a lack of real sympathy or understanding and even intense dislike for African people. This is perhaps best illustrated by his outrage with H. Drummond's exposition of the moral authority and superiority of the European over the African in *Tropical Africa* (London: Hodder & Stoughton, 1888). In his letter to James Robertson, Scott labelled Drummond's views "nonsense" and "frightful libel on humanity."⁵¹

However, it is precisely on this point, and perhaps naïvely that his high esteem for the African failed to come to terms with the epistemological implications of universalizing modern culture. Whereas Paul was willing to trust the transforming power of the gospel to other epistemological constructs,⁵² Scott's epistemological vehicle was modern culture, albeit in fertilization with African culture. It is in fusing the evangelizing and civilizing mandates that this campaigner of the equal humanity of the African unwittingly tied the African's humanity with his or her ability to be Christianized and civilized in keeping with the canons of modern culture.

This indictment is also appropriate for the source of Scott's ideas, the venerable David Livingstone. As in the case of Duff in Calcutta, civilizing became a tool for moving people away from their epistemological, cultural and social centre, irrespective of the civilizers' impeccable commitment to the honour and well-being of the natives. It practically amounted to converting Africans to both Christianity and Western rationality. The tragedy of this indictment is that those who wished to divorce evangelism from civilization were usually those with very unflattering views about the cultures, social structures and even intellectual abilities of the natives.

Ross has shown that the inspiration behind views that advocated the preservation of African cultures was a very low view of African capabilities and

---

49. 1887 to 1891 saw an increase in the number of recruits, most of whom were personally connected to Scott. Ross, *Blantyre Mission*, 24.
50. Scott to Robertson, 20 December 1880, EUL Ms. 717/10.
51. Scott to James Robertson, 14 October 1881, EUL Ms. 717/10.
52. 1 Corinthians 2:1–16; Romans 1:14–17.

even distaste for any breakdown of cultural distinctions.[53] He has also shown this to be the reason that modern African nationalists have been suspicious of those who would insist on the preservation of the integrity of African cultures, a position that was part of the foundation for apartheid.[54] We have also seen how Mbiti has incorporated the languages of former colonial masters as a part of the mosaic of post-colonial African languages, many of them in modified forms.[55]

None of the above takes anything away from the fact that, since the advent of the civilizing mandate, Africans have increasingly been on a learning curve that takes them away from their philosophical and socio-cultural ontology in a process that is more exorcism and reprogramming than it is fertilization. This is the case because the fundamental prerequisite of fertilization, the equal and mutual esteem of each other's ontology, has been lacking except for the odd radical voice. The predominant paradigm has been that of a "superior" ontology – Modern/Indo-European culture – transforming an "inferior" ontology into something "better." It is hardly surprising that the abandonment of the "inferior" ontology has taken precedence over any notions of fertilization.

However, Scott's belief in the dignity and potential of Africans was deep enough to make him one of, if not the most, culturally sensitive and empowering missionaries of his era. No other missionary in Central Africa entered into the lives of the natives more. Scott participated and presided over local judicial assemblies, the *mlandu*, a preserve of tribal leaders. In so doing, he entered into the intricate workings of the Mang'anja to a degree that none of his colleagues before him and after him did. This fact is borne out by his fine feel for Nyanja idiom in his *Cyclopaedic Dictionary of the Mang'anja*.[56]

By the confession of his successor,

> His intense faith in the possibilities of the African made them turn to him in their difficulties and troubles, and won their confidence . . . He was at his best facing a native gathering for the settlement of some case in dispute between neighbouring villages, or for the explanation of some mission plan or policy affecting the natives themselves . . . He was the incarnation of the spirit of the mission; and the Blantyre Mission to this day [1931], among the

---

53. *Blantyre Mission*, 65.
54. Ross, *Blantyre Mission*, 66.
55. Mbiti, *African Religions & Philosophy*, 101.
56. Hetherwick, *The Romance of Blantyre*, 36; Ross, *Blantyre Mission*, 70–71.

variety of mission agencies now in the country, is often and best known as "Mission wa [of] Scott," "Scott's Mission."[57]

Scott had the genius to realise that in tense, in narrative tense, in moods of the verb and in the derivation of a word from its root poetical idea, the Mang'anja language could not be judged by Western conventions:[58]

> The language moves on, gathers up all its laggards, keeps count of all its treasure, leaves "not a hoof behind." It is quite unlike the clothed and encumbered ruler of the world, – it is girded and lithe for service. It is like its equatorial palms rather than the temperate beeches, *like ideas in grass and bush rather than permanence in stone. It is "without law" to them that are "with law,"* and keeps the balance of this rocking world straight and true (italics mine).[59]

In this he was ahead of his time in recognizing that language flows from the dynamic ontology of a society:

> To any who see and really can interpret spiritual indications, African life is the true counterpart of African speech . . . It has the fullest expression of the abstract one has yet met with; it is broad and delicate in its conceptions, essentially *suaviter in modo, fortiter in re* . . . What strikes one born in all the formulas of civilisation, environed by formulas theological, social, political – which, like a veil, conceal the vision of truth – is the living touch of Bantu speech with its root ideas. It speaks from nature, but it speaks from God.[60]

Yet, even in this illustrious piece of work, it is evident that brilliant insight is tempered with a scientific approach to language and grammar. This is evident in his emphasis on rules, preceded by words like "always," in his section on the phonology of the Mang'anja language. He even has rules for the manner in which consonants combine. In a word, this is the legacy of scientism on language theory that made abstract objectivism take precedence over life-

---

57. Hetherwick, *The Romance of Blantyre*, 35–36.
58. Scott, *Cyclopaedic Dictionary of the Mang'anja*, xvii–xxi.
59. Scott, *Cyclopaedic Dictionary of the Mang'anja*, xxi.
60. Scott, *Cyclopaedic Dictionary of the Mang'anja*, xxii. See also J. G. Machen, *New Testament Greek for Beginners* (Englewood Cliffs: Prentice Hall, 1923), 3.

world, an approach that has since been disrobed in developments in language theory in the twentieth century and beyond.[61]

Scott permitted and often presided over African cultural dances and games at a time when this was hardly countenanced by other missions.[62] His weekly tea parties at the manse were also a forum for mutual brainstorming with senior boys or girls.[63] He facilitated the exposure of Malawi youths to educational facilities abroad. For example, Nacho, whom he took with him to Scotland at his own expense, helped him prepare his *Dictionary*, while acquiring some Scottish education. Several other youths were sent to Lovedale and Scotland for training.[64] His philosophy was in keeping with industrial mission:

> The trader and the missionary would liberate the producers of Africa and Asia. The pull of the industrial economy, the prestige of British ideas and technology would draw them also into the Great Commercial Republic of the World. In time the "progressive" native groups within the decaying societies of the Orient would burst the feudal shackles and liberalise their political and economic life. Thus the early Victorians hoped to help the Oriental, African and Aborigine to help themselves.[65]

Scott was ahead of his time in seeing the future of the church in Africa. In keeping with the ideas of Venn in West Africa, he strove towards a church that would be African. This could only be if the whole wealth of the Christian past was brought before the African people, from which they could select materials for their own building:

> Our purpose we lay down as the foundation of all our work that we are building the African Church – not Scotch or English – but

---

61. Scott, *Cyclopaedic Dictionary of the Mang'anja*, viii-x. See H. Gadamer, *Truth and Method* (London: Sheed & Ward, 1975), 218-19, 250-51; L. Wittgenstein, *Philosophical Investigations* (1936-49) (Oxford: Blackwell, 1967), 247; A. C. Thiselton, *New Horizons in Hermeneutics: The Theory and Practice of Transforming Biblical Reading* (London and New York: Harper Collins, 1992), 181. For a discussion of how life-world can also be tyrannical and misleading, see my treatment of James Barr's misgivings about considerations of a Hebraic mind-set in the Biblical Theology Movement in "The Exegetical Value of an African Reading of Genesis 4" (MCS Thesis, Regent College, 2000), 74-87.

62. Ross, *Blantyre Mission*, 75.

63. "Later in the 1890s this became a meeting of the senior African staff and their wives, Scott's 'deacons,' whom he hoped would be leaders of a new African church." Ross, *Blantyre Mission*, 75.

64. Ross, *Blantyre Mission*, 80-81.

65. R. Robinson and J. Gallagher, *Africa and the Victorians: the Official Mind of Imperialism* (London: Macmillan, 1961), 3-4.

African. Rather we should say the African portion of the "one Catholik and Apostolik Church." The African has a role to play in the Church of Christ universal. His character and his influence have still to be reckoned with.[66]

Towards this, he introduced Nyanja as the language of the primary service of worship for the Blantyre congregation, a position hardly appreciated by some of the missionaries and many of the settlers.[67] He went as far as putting two missionary ladies in stations under the authority of African evangelists.[68]

However, Scott's liberal approach grew increasingly unpopular with those beyond his immediate circle of influence. Among the mounting grievances against him were the following: the matter of giving African evangelists authority over European women;[69] his project of consulting with a group of African ministers in training under his tutelage in matters pertaining to the running of the mission;[70] his liberty in permitting African cultural expressions like dancing and drumming;[71] ignoring the need for the adoption of new names upon baptism by Africans;[72] and his reluctance to impose "isms," including introspective Augustinianism and Westernism, by which he meant the whole Western tradition of Christianity.[73]

When changes in the staffing of the mission tipped the balance in favour of those who disapproved, the stage was set for local and Scottish retribution. From Scotland it came in the form of threats for drastic reduction in financial support from doctrinally low church supporters of the mission.[74] Locally, the opposition was from missionaries who were incensed that Scott supervised the work with the aid of a consultative body of African deacons, contrary to the practice in other mission stations where the Mission Councils with their exclusive memberships of ordained and medical white missionaries were the real power.[75]

---

66. Scott, *Life and Work in British Central Africa*, April 1895.
67. Ross, *Blantyre Mission*, 148.
68. Ross, *Blantyre Mission*, 150.
69. Ross, *Blantyre Mission*, 150–51.
70. Ross, *Blantyre Mission*, 152–53.
71. Ross, *Blantyre Mission*, 153.
72. Ross, *Blantyre Mission*, 155–56.
73. Ross, *Blantyre Mission*, 155–56. See also D. C. Scott to Robertson, 16 December 1893, EUL Ms. 717/10.
74. McMurtie to D. C. Scott, 15 June 1893, Convenor's Letter Book, M.1. Cited in Ross, *Blantyre Mission*, 158.
75. Ross, *Blantyre Mission*, 159.

The firming of the social evolutionary theory in Europe merely exacerbated the situation. As in post-Venn West Africa, the estimation of the nature and capabilities of Africans nosedived. They were now profiled as lazy, rascally, stupid and morally decadent by default.[76] Edinburgh whittled down the authority and liberties of field missionaries: "Detailed interference with the way he was to conduct the work and even what he was to say and publish now began to press on David Clement Scott."[77]

Scott's resignation was inevitable and came in January 1898. Like Crowther in the face of the pressure of anti-African liberties' sentiment, Scott left a physically and emotionally broken man and died soon after. "His dream of an African Church, free from Western sectarianism, was apparently stifled by men who could only see the Church grow in terms of Scottish Presbyterianism."[78]

Alexander Hetherwick took over with a second reconstitution mandate: to control the "damage" inflicted by the legacy of Scott.[79] Scott's departure coincided with the expansion of British interests in the region. A British Consul for the Regions of the Shire Highlands and Lake Nyassa was appointed at the close of 1883. He was accredited to the Kings and Chiefs of Central Africa:

> His duties were to watch and report upon the slave trade in that region, and also doubtless to keep a watchful eye on the small but growing community in the Shire Highlands, and on the shores of Lake Nyasa. His presence was welcome, in as much as it gave token interest in that territory, to which its exploration by Livingstone had given her the rights of a first discoverer.[80]

However, it was the combined menace of Arab slavers and Portuguese interests from Mozambique, combined with pressure on the Prime Minister at home from representatives of the churches of Scotland, that led to the

---

76. See *The Central Africa Planter*, vol. 1, no. 8, April 1896.

77. Ross, *Blantyre Mission*, 162.

78. Ross, *Blantyre Mission*, 118, 166–67.

79. "Hetherwick never achieved the close personal relations with Africans that Scott did, and never was so passionately and understandingly negrophile as was Scott." Ross, *Blantyre Mission*, 126. In fact, in a letter at the time of Scott's death in 1907, Hetherwick is critical of Scott for being too trusting towards Africans. Hetherwick to F. Morrison Bryle, 1 October 1907, Hetherwick Files, Malawi Arch; cited in Ross, *Blantyre Mission*, 127. Also see his snide remark in the context of what was supposed to be a glowing tribute in *The Romance of Blantyre*: "At times indeed his over-confidence in the native was taken advantage of, and he was led to champion those who were unworthy of his trust" (35).

80. Hetherwick, *The Romance of Blantyre*, 47. "From 1898 onwards the Administration expanded its sphere and began to operate effectively in what is now the Central Region of Malawi and after 1904 in the northern region." Ross, *Blantyre Mission*, 126.

annexation of the territory which in terms of initial act, may be dated to the hoisting of the Union Jack in Chiromo, on 9 August 1889. The official proclamation in Nyasaland came on 21 September 1889 and in July 1891 Consul Johnston Returned to Nyasaland as Commissioner to take over the actual administration of the new Protectorate.[81]

Mission was now part of the imperial establishment. At the 1910 Missionary Conference at Mvera, the two presbyteries of Blantyre and Livingstonia formally decided to unite and form one Synod, that of the Church of Central Africa Presbyterian (CCAP).[82] The Union Nyanja Bible project represented this union in Bible translation terms.[83] Not surprisingly, European members of the CCAP continued to answer to their home churches and two Kirk Sessions, one European and one African, were formed.[84]

---

81. Heatherwick, *The Romance of Blantyre*, 67–71.

82. "However, it was not until 1914 that the slow process was completed of getting the agreement of the Church of Scotland and the, by then, United Free Church of Scotland, to this union." Ross, *Blantyre Mission*, 176–77.

83. However, the Union Nyanja project included other Missions: the Dutch Reformed Church whose headquarters were at Mvera; the Zambesi Industrial Mission; the Nyasa Industrial Mission; the Baptist Industrial Mission; and the South African General Mission. "These bodies agreed to form a Federated Board of Missions. This would consult over things such as education, Bible translation and other matters of common interest." Ross, *Blantyre Mission*, 179. See also *Historical Catalogue*, II, 2, 1165.

84. Ross, *Blantyre Mission*, 177, 179; see also W. P. Livingstone, *A Prince of Missionaries: Alexander Hetherwick* (London: James Clarke, 1931), 177–78.

10

Language and Translation Work

Missionaries were the sole architects of the education that took place in Central Africa. "Missionaries" includes the Xhosa evangelists whose idea of education was that which they had undergone at Lovedale. Many of the volunteers that responded to the invitation to join Livingstonia Mission were among the most able students, or recent graduates of Lovedale.[1]

Lovedale was a multiracial institution right up to the 1870s. It was also inter-denominational. The education offered was of a highly classical nature – with both Latin and Greek being taught, and was supplemented with manual labour as a compulsory part of the curriculum.[2] Shadrach Mngunana, the Xhosa in charge of the first official school at Livingstonia, basically passed on his Lovedale educational experience from the very beginning.[3] This state of uncontested agency also applied to the many linguistic and translation efforts that were soon the preserve of any one who had a mind to attempt it.

Apart from the examples of Laws and Riddel already encountered above, others include Mr. J. W. Moir, co-founder of the Livingstonia Central Africa Trading Company. On a business trip into modern day eastern Zambia in July 1879, accompanied by Koyi, "as a good Presbyterian layman he was keen to try his hand at a bit of Bible translation. One practical reason for this was to help with the prayers and worship services which were regularly held on such journeys."[4]

In what amounts to a Journal kept by Moir, we see him "busy all afternoon translating the word God had given us into Manganja language . . . We [with

---

1. Thompson, *Touching the Heart*, 8.

2. Thompson, *Touching the Heart*, 9–10; Lovedale Annual Report 1872–88, General Regulations, 4, cited p. 10.

3. Thompson, *Touching the Heart*, 37–38.

4. Thompson, *Touching the Heart*, 89–90.

Koyi] have nearly completed the fourth chapter of Mark since we started on this journey."[5] The entry for Wednesday and Thursday 12 and 13 August has Moir preaching and the two of them translating. "Last Sunday morning, I addressed another meeting on the woman of Samaria; and William and I finished the translation of Mark, which we commenced on Tuesday, 8 July, soon after starting on this journey."

Under the entry entitled "Kaningina Station, Sunday, August 31, 1879," he records that "Koyi and I finished our second revision of Acts by reading it over to two or three of our best Manganja boys . . . I think it is pretty fair now. I do trust it may be blessed and owned of God." Under the entry for Kaningina, Tuesday 2 September, Moir partly discloses how he went about acquiring his translation skills. "I have been working away pretty hard at the language, chiefly in going over the little vocabulary we have, with a number of manuscript additions I copied at Blantyre, adding words, and new and varied meanings to many of the native words."[6]

The progress of language and translation work that occurred in Old Calabar is generally replicated here. Missionaries, irrespective of skill, collected vernacular words, memorized them, then attempted to simplify and systematize their orthography. Laws captures this freedom to translate among missionaries very well:

> For a long time I hesitated to begin a translation of the Word of God in a new language which we knew imperfectly; but others, considerably less prepared, were not deterred by a similar sense of responsibility, so that I finally decided to undertake the task. Repeatedly I tackled the translation, but before reaching the end of the Gospel, I was so dissatisfied with the errors made that I invariably began it all over again.[7]

When Margaret Laws, the former Margaret Gray, joined her husband at Cape Maclear, she apparently was the one who reduced the Chinyanja language to writing although Laws seems to get all the credit.[8]

---

5. Entry reading "TEMBWE'S WASENGA COUNTRY, *Sunday, July 20, 1879.*"

6. "Lake Nyassa – Letters of Mr J. W. Moir," *The Christian Express* (June 1880): 5–6. James Stewart CE's journal bears a hand-written translation of the Lord's Prayer by Laws into chiMang'anja that he apparently carried with him to aid him with his church services during his travels. Thompson, *From Nyassa to Tanganyika*, 33.

7. *Reminiscences of Livingstonia*, 130.

8. AUL Spec. Coll. Ms 3290/3. Notes by Miss A. N. Laws on her father, cited in McIntosh, *Robert Laws*, 4. A small booklet including Hymns, in the native language, dated 1879–82, and

The empirical process was the method of choice. In the words of Laws,

> At first all the sounds were strange to us and we had difficulty in recognising them. We wrote down what we heard, and it was interesting in later years to see the mistakes we had made, frequently splitting one word into two, attaching the first half to the preceding word, and the second half to the following word. With practice the crudest mistakes were soon eliminated, but it takes much time and patience, also close contact with the natives, to grasp the true idiom of a language. Even with the greatest effort, diligence and perseverance, it seems almost impossible for a European to get at the real inner meaning of the native mind.[9]

Moir's and Koyi's translation of Mark was the first to be completed.[10]

It was common practice to test the comprehensibility of what was translated on locals. In Laws' case, this meant selecting the most competent pupils in the mission schools to help him with his translation of the New Testament. The work thus produced would then be read at public worship daily with a plea for feedback from the natives as to the quality of the translations. Further, some of the older pupils often borrowed his manuscripts and read them out in the villages in the afternoons, explaining their meaning to the people.[11]

The initial decision to translate into Nyanja was apparently made by Laws and for selfish reasons:

> Nyanja was spoken in the Shire Highlands and at some of the villages at Cape Maclear, whereas Yao was the predominating language at Mponda, the chief village at the south end of the Lake, also at most of the neighbouring villages. In Nyanja there is no difficult sound foreign to the English, language, and the structure is simpler than in Yao.[12]

However, this decision had its pragmatic side.

> Lake Nyasa is 360 miles long, yet round that Lake six languages are spoken – some of them in two or three different dialects, and this without counting the languages among the peoples in the

---

with the initials "ML" attached and an early reader in Mrs Laws' handwriting are evidences of her labour. EUL, Laws' Coll. Gen. 561/7; Gen. 561/11.

9. *Reminiscences of Livingstonia*, 127–28.
10. Laws, *Reminiscences of Livingstonia*, 130.
11. Laws, *Reminiscences of Livingstonia*, 131; NLS 7910, Kan. Journal 24/8/1879.
12. Laws, *Reminiscences of Livingstonia*, 127.

Highlands to the east and west and north of the Lake. Of the nine stations occupied as European centres by the Livingstonia Mission, only three use the same language. At each of the other six, a separate language is used by the people among whom the station is situated. It can be easily seen that to provide anything like a literature in each of these languages is practically impossible, even if it were desirable. The suggestion was therefore made to choose a rather widespread language to be used as a *lingua franca* for the whole Lake District. Nyanja, which is spoken not only in the Shire Highlands, but in a great part of the west side of the Lake, also at its southern end, seemed to be most suitable.[13]

He notes, however, that the status of Nyanja as lingua franca did not extend to northern regions where Livingstonia Mission later relocated. Here Nyanja was totally rejected and fresh translation work into local languages like Tumbuka had to be done.[14] However, the demand for English as an instrument towards economic wellbeing, on the evidence of those who already acquired it, soared. In the words of Laws,

Whatever may be said with regard to the advisability of preserving the native languages, no one with practical experience of work in many districts of Central Africa will hesitate to agree that the sooner many of these different languages become extinct, the better for the peace, prosperity, and the advancement of the country and its people. To the young in these regions, English is practically synonymous with progress.[15]

Like Waddell in Calabar, the collection of native linguistic material preceded the entrance of the mission. In this case, pre-entrance linguistic help included the acquisition of one or two vocabularies formed many years prior by the Universities Mission when they operated at Magomero, and a dictionary published by a Mr Rebman of Momba. It also included securing the services of several boys who had been set free by Dr. Livingstone from a slave gang and taken by Horace Walker to Cape Town when Bishop Tozer removed the Universities Mission from Magomero to Zanzibar. One of these boys was a

---

13. Laws, *Reminiscences of Livingstonia*, 132–33.
14. Laws, *Reminiscences of Livingstonia*, 133.
15. Laws, *Reminiscences of Livingstonia*, 134.

fluent Nyanja speaker; the others understood Nyanja, but knew Yao better.[16] The task of reducing the language to writing was controlled by the same dynamics as in Calabar. In terms of adopting an alphabet (morphology), usually through a correlation of sound to an Indo-European literary symbol, delineating its grammar, and attempting to ascertain its syntax, the missionaries were totally in charge. The involvement of the natives was confined to experimentation with the finished product.

A synopsis of Scripture translations into Western and Eastern Nyanja made during this period reveals the prolific nature of this enterprise. With respect to Western Nyanja, *African Scriptures*, Vol. II includes: Mark (1880) by Laws, printed at Lovedale and lost in a raid by the Machinjiri en route to Cape Maclear; St. John (1881) by Laws; Matthew (1885) by Laws; Mark (1885) by Laws; Luke (1885) by Laws; the New Testament (1886) by Laws; Genesis (1893) by G. Henry of the Free Church of Scotland Mission; Esther (1894) by A. C. Murray of the Dutch Reformed Church Mission; a revision of Matthew (1898) by Laws; and a revision of Mark (1898) by Laws.[17]

To this the *Historical Catalogue*, II, 2 adds a revision of the Gospels and Acts (1899) by Laws and a revision of the New Testament (1900) by Laws.[18] With respect to Southern Nyanja, *African Scriptures*, Vol. II includes a booklet containing Scripture selections (1881) by Scott; Matthew (1892) by Scott; Mark (1892) by Scott; Luke (1893) by Scott; John (1893) by Scott; and Ephesians, Philippians and Colossians (1894) by Scott.[19] With respect to Union Nyanja, *African Scriptures*, Vol. II, includes Matthew (1901) by the Nyanja Bible Translation Committee under the chairmanship of Hetherwick; the New Testament (1906) prepared by W. H. Murray of the Dutch Reformed Church Mission; Psalms (1911) prepared by the Nyanja Bible Translation Committee; the Bible (1922) translated by the Union Nyanja Translation Committee – W. H. being assisted by R. H. Napier, C. S. M., and Che Ndombe; and a new edition of the Bible (1936) printed in accordance with new orthographical rules drawn up by W. H. Murray.[20] Scripture translations into Union Nyanja continue beyond this point but we will stop here for the purposes of this book.

---

16. Laws, *Reminiscences of Livingstonia*, 127; McIntosh, *Robert Laws*, 81; FCGA Reports 1884, 102.
17. *African Scriptures*, Vol. II, 529–31.
18. *Historical Catalogue*, II, 1157.
19. *African Scriptures*, Vol. II, 528–29.
20. *African Scriptures*, Vol. II, 533–34.

We have also omitted the vast material classified under Eastern Nyanja because it is not a part of the Union Nyanja project.

Union Nyanja was in part an amalgamation of several original efforts that were edited, and at times retranslated by the Union Nyanja Bible Translation Committee. In the evaluation of M. W. Retief:

> Before 1900, the Livingstonia Mission of the Free Church of Scotland had the New Testament, but it was a poor translation. The Blantyre Mission of the Established Church of Scotland had the four Gospels but the translation of these was not suitable for use by those of the other missions. The question then arose whether a translation of the Bible could be made into Cinyanja which could be used by all the missions at work in Nyasaland. After a good deal of discussion of, and correspondence on the subject, the first meeting of the Cinyanja Bible Translation Commission took place at Fort Johnson in May of 1900. There were present Dr. Hetherwick of the Blantyre Mission (Chairman), the Rev. Mr. McAlpine of the Livingstonia-Mission, the Rev. Mr. Blake and the Rev. A. C. Murray of the Dutch Reformed Church Mission. Mr. Murray acted as secretary. They decided at that meeting to undertake a new translation of the Bible into Cinyanja which all the Cinyanja-speaking people of the country would be able to use. The method of procedure with regard to the translation was also discussed and they drew up a glossary of about 140 Bible terms in Cinyanja, on the meaning of which they were all agreed and which would serve as a guide to the translators from the various missions.[21]

In this book, we will focus on one of the original efforts, Laws' translation of Mark, for our case study. We will thereafter compare this translation with Scott's 1893 translation and the 1922 Union Nyanja edition of the same text in order to throw some light on the missionaries' epistemological hegemony and the levels of African agency in the two projects.

---

21. M. W. Retief, *William Murray of Nyasaland*, translated by Mary H. Le Roux and M. M. Oberholster-Le Roux (Cape Town: The Lovedale Press, 1958), 96; Laws, *Reminiscences of Livingstonia*, 132.

Figure 4. The Rev. Dr. Robert Laws, Livingstonia Mission.[22]

Laws' Theory of Language and Translation Procedures

As the leader of Livingstonia Mission and its medical officer, Laws was well placed to engage in close contact with the natives. An ordained minister, he was well qualified to relate language and translation to both the evangelizing and civilizing mandates. Yet his comments on the subject of language theory and translation reveal an interest that scarcely exceeded pragmatic concerns.

Laws practically gave up on the possibility of ever getting at "the real inner meaning of the native mind."[23] He obviously envisaged the day when English would be universally spoken in the Shire Highlands, a prospect that

---

22. H. McIntosh, *Robert Laws* (Carberry, Scotland: The Handsel Press, 1993), 20. Image used by permission.

23. Laws, *Reminiscences of Livingstonia*, 128.

he, through his "practical experience," saw as "better for the peace, prosperity and the advancement of the country and its people."[24]

Here, we do not find Scott's philosophical commitment to the development of Africa and Africans through a fertilization of cultures. We already saw how Laws' choice of Nyanja over Yao was partly influenced by Nyanja's phonological familiarity to the English ear. He chose Mark as the first Gospel to translate because it was the shortest and simplest of the Gospels and, "to a large extent, free from reference to the beliefs or conditions of life amongst both Jews and Gentiles, such as are to be found in other Gospels."[25]

Laws arrived in Central Africa quite ignorant of the syntax and grammar of African languages and depended on his knowledge of European languages and the Classics in trying to delineate them and reduce them to writing. To his credit, he was able to recognize that "the Hebrew causative was the only thing that threw any light on African languages." His frustration is evident in his account of an encounter with the strangeness of the language. "It was difficult to get any satisfactory explanation with regard to the peculiarities of the language; for our interpreter, who acted as teacher, invariably answered, 'That is just how it is.'"[26]

Laws was also able to realise that "the great majority of what are known as Bantu languages have their grammar based on the principle of euphonic or alliteral concord."[27] In fact, his unfamiliarity with the new languages was such that, by his own confession, he was only disposed to attempt translation when he saw that some of his colleagues, "considerably less prepared, were not deterred by a similar sense of responsibility."[28]

Laws was idealistically committed to a native church that developed along the lines of semi-independence from the home church from the very beginning. In his words,

> It is absurd to expect a Church abroad to accept the Westminster Confession of Faith as its standard, even if it could be adequately translated into the native language. The environment of the people is quite different; the circumstances they have to face are also different; and it is out of place to burden a new Church with

---

24. Laws, *Reminiscences of Livingstonia*, 134.
25. Laws, *Reminiscences of Livingstonia*, 130.
26. Laws, *Reminiscences of Livingstonia*, 128–29.
27. Laws, *Reminiscences of Livingstonia*, 129. See Goldie's observation of this very point with respect to the Efik in *Calabar and its Mission*, 301.
28. Laws, *Reminiscences of Livingstonia*, 130.

declarations regarding the civil rights of the magistrate and the spiritual rights of the Church where no such question exists.[29]

This may partly be responsible for some of the concessions that he made towards a native initiative. For example, he allowed the native church to settle the matter of their native pastors' salaries without European interference.[30] However, H. J. Sindima has argued that Livingstonia Mission reneged on its promises to empower natives. In fact, the Christianity practised at Livingstonia has been equated to severance from one's Africanness:

> Contrary to all claims of creating an indigenous church, Livingstonia was very slow in appointing Africans to positions of authority... Livingstonia missionaries identified evangelization with Europeanization and since the Lovedale men lacked "a whole bearing of European" as Elmslie put it, the African could not be an effective missionary.[31]

Elmslie is particularly cited as the one who refused to recognize the equality of African co-workers.[32] However, he seemed to merely voice what was the silent position of his colleagues, including Laws, at Livingstonia Mission:

> They may not have overtly shown their prejudice but they surely shared the views Elmslie had about Africans. Those negative feelings were passed on to members of the Home Committee. They too seemed to have the same attitude towards Africans. What the letters and reports from Livingstonia did was to strengthen their already held views about Africans.[33]

According to Morrison, the policy of undervaluing Africans remained intact within Livingstonia throughout the period of Scottish missionary enterprise: "Missionaries held all positions of authority, made all decisions without even consulting Malawians. In almost all cases their decision was final since they considered it 'the law of Christ.'"[34] In Sindima's estimation, "the process of

---

29. Laws, *Reminiscences of Livingstonia*, 143.

30. Laws, *Reminiscences of Livingstonia*, 140. He also allowed natives, for example pastor Peter Tholi [Thole?] to write native hymns and compose tunes (141).

31. H. J. Sindima, *The Legacy of Scottish Missionaries in Malawi*, Studies in the History of Missions, Volume 8 (Lampeter, Wales: The Edwin Mellen Press, 1992), 35–36; Elmslie to Laws, 7 January 1887, NLS 7890.

32. Sindima, *The Legacy*, 36–37.

33. Sindima, *The Legacy*, 37.

34. J. H. Morrison, *Streams in the Desert: A Picture of Life in Livingstonia* (London: Doran, 1919), 47–48.

alienation became total and permanent among those who got employed by the mission as teachers, apprentices or evangelists."[35] However, where human beings are involved, involuntary subjugation can never be permanent as the tragic case of the John Chilembwe uprising of 1915 demonstrates, its circumstances and excesses notwithstanding.[36]

In spite of the countless references to translation work undertaken by Laws, we can scarcely find any references to the material that he used as the original from which to translate. This may be the case because, given his education, it is assumed that he had knowledge, access and was probably even in possession of the sort of biblical academic resources that his generation considered standard. Certainly, his wrestling with the etymology of Nyanja words in the light of English, Latin or Greek etymologies evidences awareness, if not possession of related material.[37] Yet, the silence may also adumbrate an absence of the intense and meticulous interest in linguistic study that was observable in Goldie of Old Calabar.

In all this, Livingstonia under Laws, with the qualified exception of Donald Fraser's tenure, was quite the antithesis of Blantyre Mission under Scott.[38] Given this elitist ethos and Laws' pragmatic approach to African socio-cultural practices and languages, it is not far-fetched to conclude that Laws had the final word on all translations credited to his name. Here, even more so than in the case of Goldie, any linguistic capabilities of the Africans were of no consequence apart from their use in responding to already translated material.

---

35. *The Legacy*, 73–74.

36. See K. R. Ross, ed., *Christianity in Malawi: A Source Book* (Gweru, Zimbabwe: Mambo Press, 1996), 145–54.

37. McIntosh, *Robert Laws*, 82. Also see his reference to the properties of the Hebrew causative in *Reminiscences of Livingstonia*, 129. According to Smalley's profile of the classical education of the times, Laws would have been exposed to Latin and Greek study from his secondary school years right through to university. *Translation as Mission*, 105, 106.

38. Sindima, *The Legacy*, 78–80.

11

Evaluative Commentary on Laws' Translation of Mark 1:1–8

In this chapter an analysis of actual translations will be made in order to determine, as closely as possible, the presence and effect of epistemological presuppositions in the text. To facilitate an adequate comparison of the translations, we will confine textual analysis to the first eight verses of Mark chapter one that Laws translated.

The ensuing commentary has been made in the light of the GNT text of Mark 1:1-8.[1] The detailed commentary is in the form of comment notes at the end of the book and coded to the text of Laws' translation with the corresponding page numbers below. Laws submitted his manuscript to the printer in 1885 – Morrison & Gibb, Edinburgh, printers to her Majesty's Stationery for the National Bible Society of Scotland – meaning that this translation represents about eight years' work.

The separate Gospels were submitted as *Maivangeli a Mwini Watu ndi Mpulumutsi Yesu Kristu kwa Mateyu, Marko, Luka, ndi Yohane: Mau a Tshinyanja*, Edinburgh: Printed for the National Bible Society of Sctland, 1885. They were resubmitted as part of *Testamente Watsopano wa Mwini Watu ndi Mpulumutsi Yesu Kristu: Mau a Tshinyanja*, Edinburgh: Printed for the National Bible Society of Scotland, 1885 for printing and proof-reading and published the following year as part of his New Testament.

---

1. See Appendix I.

Commentary
Verse 1

Kuamba kwa invangeli wa Yesu Kristu, Mwana wa Mulungu

Kuamba kwa
The vocalization of *kuamba* word lacks "y," in order to read *kuyamba*.

The prefix *ku* and the relative pronoun, *kwa*, which correctly stands as a reference back to **kuyamba** are inappropriate choices for "the beginning . . ." a title of the account that is to follow. The appropriate prefix is **Chi**-*yambi cha*-.

Invangeli
Invangeli is transliteration for ευαγγελιου, not translation. It is not clear where the inclusion of "n" is coming from. Perhaps Laws thought he heard this when the local pronounced it.

Verse 2

Inde monga alembedwa m'Yesaya, mprofeti
Ona dituma ntenga wanga patsogolo pa nkope yako;
Emwe adzakonzetsa njira yako;

Inde
Laws prefaces Καθως, "just as" with a word, *Inde*, that stands for emphasis, the equivalent of English "surely," "indeed," even "yes." *Monga* has already translated Καθως and it is hard to understand where *inde* is coming from.

Alembedwa
There is total misrepresentation of the tense of the verb *alembedwa*. The prefix *a* does not correspond with the stative nature of the perfect passive verb γεγραπται. To convey this idea, the translator may have to resort to the non-specific subject marker *chi*, "it [is]" as in **chi-na-lembedwa**. Alternatively, the subject may have to be mentioned specifically.

m'Yesaya
Laws has translated the locative εν τω Ησαια τω προφητη, with the prefix *m*'- that does not communicate what is being referred to. If he had translated "prophet" properly, say with the noun *m'neneri*, "one who prophesies" where *nena*, "utter speech" can be extended to indicate prophesying, the task of translating the locative would have been easy: *mu'mneneri Yesaya*. Both options would make *Yesaya* the book or scroll by that title.

Mprofeti

The office, function, and title of this rich noun are totally lost in the transliteration that Laws has adopted. See the suggestion in the comment above.

dituma

The omission of *n* at the beginning of this word renders *di-* an incomprehensible prefix where *ndi-* is the correct form for the first person singular verbal prefix.

ntenga

n is not the correct consonant for the noun for messenger. Further, the pronunciation of *t* is the aspirated form *th*. Messenger in Nyanja is *mthenga*. *Ntenga* would actually be understood as *ni-tenga* where *ni* would be a variant in some Nyanja dialects of *ndi* – "I am" (see comment above). *Tenga* means "take," leading to the meaning, "I am taking" and not "messenger."

nkope

The correct vocalization of the noun "face," *nkhope*, requires an *h* after *k*.

Emwe

The vocalization of *emwe* lacks the consonant *y* as in *yemwe*.

adzakonzetsa

Final *-etsa* is misleading as it is essentially an ending for the superlative and means "he will prepare most precisely, judiciously," etc. The future is adequately rendered by *adzakonza*.

Verse 3

Liu la modzi kulira m'tshipululu,
Fotokozani njira ya mwini
Pangani njira zatshi zolungama;

Liu ("a word") is already singular by virtue of the prefix *li-*. *La modzi* is an attempt at perpetuating this element in what he called "euphonic or alliteral concord." However, *la* is the wrong form of the supplied relative pronoun to refer back to *liu*. This would demand *li-* as in ***liu limodzi***. However, if his intention is to translate the participle Βοωντος attributively (as is perhaps more accurate given the fact that Φωνη, a feminine noun, is not modified by the masculine participle βοωντος), the *la* becomes an indication that the participle is translated in the attributive sense. However, this also demands the pronominal subject prefix *u-* (the equivalent of the Greek "ο" leading to the understanding, "the one who") before the participle as in *liu la **u**-modzi* ("a/the voice of one who . . .").

There is a better word than *kulira* for the concept of "crying out" or "calling out" in the sense of announcing a proclamation. That word is *[p]fuula*, in this case translatable as *la o[p]fuula*. *Kulira*, when used of human beings, is usually associated with weeping, mourning, sobbing etc.

m'tshipululu

Laws has consistently translated *tsh* for what should be *c[h]* as in *m'c[h]ipululu*. Perhaps this is what he thought he was hearing.

This is a total misreading of the nuance of *fotokoza*, "explain" or "elaborate." Ετοιμασατε is "prepare" or "make ready." See BAGD, 316. It has a stronger affinity with *konzani*, the imperative active indicative 2pl. of the verb *konza*, than κατασκευασει in verse 2 that was translated as *adzakonzetsa* from the same root. Perhaps he came across *fotokozani* in the context of "explaining" as in "unfolding speech," but the word is a dubious choice for the Greek word above.

Κυριος is translated as *mwini* which literally means "owner." This is a very poor translation for the Greek (or the English "Lord" for that matter). This direct quotation of LXX Isa 40:3 corresponds with פנו דרך יהוה (BHS) and just as it is difficult to imagine how פנה , literally "turn" and therefore "turn away," "put out of the way," "make clear," can be understood as *fotokozani* (BDB, 815), it is difficult to see how יהוה can be nuanced as *mwini* unless it is a theological interpretation. "Owner," *mwini* may approximate κυριος if an estate is in mind. However, it is also a very common noun for any kind of ownership and needs further qualification. *Mbuye* or *ambuye* whatever term has been agreed for translating the Hebrew יהוה is expected for κυριος here.

Pangani is more likely to be associating with "construct" in this text, than "prepare." By making *njira*, "pathways," the direct object of the verb *pangani*, he has obscured the fact that, in this double accusative construction, "straight," ευθειας, is the first accusative following the verb. This realization would then make it possible to adopt one word in Nyanja for both "make" and "straight" that has the concept of "make straight" as its root meaning, for example, *lungamitsani*. Instead, Laws has two words, *pangani . . . zolungama*, a construction that is fraught with ambiguity.

Zatshi

As was the case with *m'tshipululu*, Laws appears to be hearing *tshi* where *chi* would stand. This word should read "*zache*."

Verse 4

Yohane nadza, emwe anabapatiza m'tshipululu Nauza mbapatisma la kutembenuza ntima kwa kubweza kwa zimpulupulu.

The vocalization of *emwe* is faulty: it requires a preceding *y* to read *yemwe* for the relative pronoun "[the one] who." Further, the relative as an independent word is redundant because the subject is already indicated in the verbal prefix *na* in **nadza**. See Seow for a similar phenomenon in the Hebrew language.[2] However, it is probably the case that Laws is attempting to translate the participle [ο] βαπτιζων attributively, "the one who." See the following note for the quality of this effort.

anabapatiza

Laws is neither reading the participle [ο] βαπτιζων attributively (as the NAS), nor predicately, ignoring the article (as the NIV), but is reading what appears to be the KJV "John did baptize in the wilderness." However, the *emwe* suggests that he is trying to read it attributively although his translation of the participle suggests a verb: *anabapatiza* literally means "he baptized," expected of a regular *qal* verb.

m'tshipululu

We have already commented on this strange form.

Nauza

Na- as the subject prefix in the verb refers back to John and shows that he is reading John as the subject of the participle. However, *uza* is literally "tell" or "narrate." It is very dubious as a translation for κηρυσσων, "preaching" or "proclaiming" for which the Nyanja verb *lalikira* is more appropriate and would yield *nalalikira*.

The appropriate pronominal indicator for an impersonal noun indicating activity, and beginning with the consonant *b* is *u-* as in **uba[pa]tizo** not *m-* (a redacted form of the prefix *mu*, "in"). *Bapatisma* is undisguised and very poor transliteration of βαπτισμα (Chewa would typically require a vowel with the *s*) and with no attempt made whatsoever to translate the concept/activity. *Mbapatisma* would therefore approximate a meaning akin to "in baptism." This underscores Laws' lack of critical interaction with Nyanja words and concepts.

---

2. C. L. Seow, *A Grammar for Biblical Hebrew*, rev. ed. (Nashville: Abingdon Press, 1995), 205.

la

The lack of understanding of "euphonic or alliteral concord" in relation confusion to the prefix to the preceding noun (*mbapatisma*) is evident in the choice of relative pronoun here (as an effort at translating identity in the attributive genitive μετανοιας. *u-* would have called for the genitive case pointer *wa-* as in **ubatizo wa-**.

kutembenuza ntima

Here we have an attempt at translating the concept of repentance as "converting the heart," hence the addition of *-za* to the concept of baptism, which translates this noun into a participle, and *ntima*, "heart." To begin with, *ntima* is a faulty vocalization of the noun where *mtima* ought to stand. Second, *kutembenuza ntima* introduces a theological interpretation in the text as text, since, in his rendering, it is the baptism that converts the heart. But if μετανοιας is understood as an attributive genitive, the focus of the genitive is on answering the question "what kind of baptism?" and not on denoting the redemptive function of the baptism, a construction that would require a predicate participle taking the direct object "heart."[3] Both cited grammars describe the genitive as fundamentally the case of definition or description.

kwa

In this context, *kwa* as a translation of εἰς is intended to denote purpose. Yet the Nyanja *kwa* in this context is merely definitive, indicating "of what kind," "of what sort," "with reference to," or some such idea. It is the equivalent of translating the Greek genitive without attempting to show what sort of genitive it is here.

kubweza

Kubweza, literally "returning," is a very poor choice for αφεσις, "forgiveness" or "cancellation," or "pardon."[4] If Laws had "remission" in mind, then he has used a word that is quite devoid of the idea of "guilt" in it and that begs the question of what is meant by "returning sins." *Bweza* is commonly used of "returning" as a very normative and virtuous undertaking: people return items that they borrowed from friends, etc.

---

3. See C. Vaughan and V. E. Gideon, *A Greek Grammar of the New Testament* (Nashville : Broadman Press, 1979), 31; H. E. Dana and J. R. Mantey, *A Manual Grammar of the Greek New Testament* (Toronto, Ontario: Macmillan, 1957), 72.

4. BAGD, 125.

zimpulupulu
Zi- is a strange marker of plurality for the word *mphulupulu* ("sin") that stands both in the singular and the plural: a collective singular noun. Notice the omission of *h* in Laws' vocalization.

Verse 5

Ndimo naturuka kwa ie dziko lonse la Yudeya, ndi onse omwe a Yerusalem; ndimo nabapatizidwa ndi ie m'ntsinje Yordan, kubvumbula zimpulupulu zao.

Ndimo (x2)

Ndimo, literally "that is how," is Laws' rendering of και, instead of the appropriate *ndipo*.

naturuka

The prefix *na-* does not agree with the pronominal particle *lo-* in *lonse* and the genitive marker *la* referring to the subject of this verb, *dziko*. Actually, *na-* is serving as a tense marker here. To achieve such agreement requires the addition of *li-* to the verb: *linaturuka kwa iye dziko lonse la Yudeya*. Further, *turuka*, literally "come out" or "emerge" is a graphic but needs to be supplemented by the notion of "travelling," something like "come out and go to[wards]," as in *linaturu-kira*. However, *turuka* sounds like someone trying to get an equivalent for the English "came out" and is not natural Chewa.

ie (x2)

It is quite inconceivable that a word without any consonant could stand in Chewa. *Iye* would be the appropriate word here.

omwe

Omwe is redundant preceding *a* which likewise functions here as the definite article in οι Ιερυσολυμιται as well as an indicator of the element of "inhabitants of" inherent in the noun Ιεροσολυμιται. However, the *a* needs to be complemented with the pronominal prefix *mu-* (in) as in *onse* [all] *a mu Yerulasemu*." Notice the Bantu vocalization of "Jerusalem" and how it differs from Laws' vocalization even though both are transliterations of the name of the city. His transliteration lacks a vowel at the end. In addition, Laws has made the choice to transliterate the Hebrew *yod* (y) using "y" and not "j" as in English translations.

m'ntsinje

Mtsinje is the Nyanja noun for "river," "stream" etc. But notice the faulty vocalization by Laws, namely, **ntsinje**. He has correctly tried to indicate the locative εν τω Ιορδανη ποταμω by the prefixed preposition *m'*- but this prefix, standing before a word beginning with the consonant *m*, must be vocalized *mu*- as in **mumtsinje**. Since *yorodane* (notice my deliberate vocalization in this transliteration of the name compared to his 'Yordan') stands in apposition to *mtsinje*, there is need to indicate this with a reference marker, *wa* as in **mumtsinje wa Yorodane**.

kubvumbula

Kubvumbula, "uncovering," is problematic for two reasons. First, it does not indicate the subject of this activity because its form is the equivalent of the Greek predicate infinitive. A pronominal prefix like *ali-*, "as/while they are/were," must be supplied to indicate this. Yet, more critically, the noun itself is quite inappropriate for conveying the middle voice in εξομολογουμενοι. This requires a root like *lapila* or a paraphrase that indicates acknowledgement of culpability in the idea of "uncovering." See the English "confess."

zimpulupulu

The prefix *zi*- is probably meant to be a plural marker and also intended to go with the *z* in the form of the third person genitive plural personal pronoun **zao**. Recall Laws' confession that he routinely sought to achieve euphonic or alliteral concord: "I had to learn that the great majority of what are known as Bantu languages have their grammar based on the principle of euphonic or alliteral concord."[5] However, *zao* is correct and stands even when we alter the form of the noun to *mphulupulu*. *Mphulupulu* ("sins") can be both singular and plural and does not require the prefix *zi*. Further, he omits *h* in his spelling of the noun.

Verse 6

Ndimo Yohane wabvala ndi ubwea wa gamila, nali ndi lamba la tshikopa m'tshunu mwatshi, ndimo nadia madzombe ndi utshi wa muntengo.

Ndimo

See commentary on this word in verse 5.

---

5. Laws, *Reminiscences of Livingstonia*, 129.

wabvala

The prefix *wa-* denotes the present tense of the verb and is not the appropriate aspect for Nyanja narrative (as the controlling idea). As Scott also observed with respect to the narrative tense,

> just as in Hebrew, an action once stated in its proper time throws the halo of that time round all the clauses dependent upon it in thought; and the verbs of these clauses accordingly take a simple present with the gentle *"vav*-conversive" *n* or *ni: iye a-na-dza, na-nena, na-nenabe, na-pita na-enda*, he came and speaks and speaks on, and passes and goes on his way.[6]

This requires an initial *ana-* as in *anabvala*, etc. This construction will also make the following *ndi* redundant. Obviously Laws is struggling to translate the KJV "clothed with" using the literal *wabvala ndi* for the perfect participle ενδεδυμενος.

ubwea

Needs a consonant in order to be vocalized as *ubweya* ("hair").

gamila

Apparently, Laws was not hearing the initial *n* as this should be vocalized as *ngamila* ("camel").

nali

What seems to be the text here is, again, the KJV "and with girdle of skin" and *nali* is supposed to correspond with the English "[clothed] with." However, *nali* means "had" or "was with," a construction that is not in the Greek text. The text shows και ζωνην δερματινην to be governed by the one participle, ενδεδυμενος. In the light of comment above on *wabvala*, this means that *anabvala* governs both *ubweya wa ngamila* and *lamba* with the conjunction *ndi*, και supplied to indicate this.

la

The fact that the noun *lamba* begins with *la-* does not mean that its referent will be *la*. In fact, *lamba* elicits *wa* as its genitive referent. The legendary Union

---

6. Scott, *A Cyclopaedic Dictionary of the Mang'anja*, xviii. See also Seow, *A Grammar for Biblical Hebrew*, 226–27; S. Bar-Efrat, *Narrative Art in the Bible*, 2nd ed., Bible and Literature Series 17 (Sheffield: Academic Press, 1984), 165–67.

Nyanja Version, *Buku Lopatuluka*, made the same error.[7] However, its revision much later, *Buku Loyera*, changed the referent prefix to the belt from *la* to *wa*.[8]

tshikopa
The challenge of hearing the sound *ts* instead of *c* continues. *Cikopa*, as also the *Buku Lopatulika* has it, is the correct rendering.

m'tshunu
This is a difficult noun to vocalize because it features a syllable, *u* that is a single vowel: *chi/u/no*, "waist." This is a rare occurrence in this language and it is understandable that Laws totally missed the double *u-u* or *i-u* sounds here. *m'-* is an appropriate rendering for περι followed by an accusative. But we see his persistent error in vocalizing *ch-* or *c* as *tsh*.

mwatshi
Should read *mwache* or *mwace*.

ndimo
See commentary in verse 5 above on this wording.

nadia
This noun is di-syllabic not tri-syllabic: *na/dya* not *na/di/a*. The root for "eating" is *dya* and the prefix *na-* is the narrative tense prefix alluded to by Scott that shows, among other things, John the Baptist to be the subject of εσθιων.

madzombe
The noun *dzombe*, "locusts," like *mphulupulu*, is a collective singular noun and therefore does not need the prefix *ma-* to render it in the plural sense.

utshi
The challenge of hearing *tsh* where *ch* or *c* should be heard continues. "Honey" is vocalized *uchi* or *uci*. In this particular case, his errant vocalization is dangerously misleading because *utsi*, obtained by merely dropping an *h* from his spelling, is a very different noun meaning "smoke" as in the smoke of burning material such as grass.

---

7. *Buku Lopatulika ndilo Mau a Mulungu: Chipangano cha Kale ndi cha Tsopano*. Translated by the Union Nyanja Translation Committee (Edinburgh: National Bible Society of Scotland and British and Foreign Bible Society, 1922). Revised in 1966.

8. *Buku Loyera* (Blantyre, Malawi: The Bible Society of Malawi), 1998.

muntengo
The vocalization of the noun for "wild," *ntengo*, should be *thengo*, literally "bush." *M'tengo* is a different noun meaning "tree." If Laws had the correct noun, he would have needed to add the prefix *mu* (with the *u* elided, giving *m'-*), the equivalent of the English "in," to indicate the accusative of reference μελι αγριον, *uchi wa m'thengo*. Consequently, Laws' choice here is fraught with confusion.

Verse 7

Ndimo nauza, kuti, Alinkudza pambuiu pa ine iemwe ali wampamvu wopambana ine, zingwe za dzikwatakwata dzatshi sindiri woenera ku weramira ku masula.

Ndimo
See the commentary on this word in verse 5 above.

nauza
See the commentary above (v. 4) concerning the problem of translating κηρυσσω with *uza*.

kuti
A better way of translating the participle introducing direct speech, λεγων, would be *nati* because the subject in the participle is evident in the prefix *na-* whereas *kuti* is more appropriate for the introduction of direct speech by the impersonal οτι.

Alinkudza
The introduction of *n* in *alinkudza* is quite inexplicable. *aliku-*, or simply *aku-* "he is/will be," are the prefixes indicating the third person singular future indicative for the verb root *dza*, "coming." *Adza* would be even smoother as also the fuller *alikubwera* or *abwera* where the synonym *bwera*, "coming," is used.[9]

pambuiu
Mbuiu is a gross vocalization (or hearing) error of *mbuyo*, "behind." Read *pambuyo*.

---

9. Note that where the translators of *Buku Lopatulika* went with the root *dza*, the translators of *Buku Loyera* opted for the root *bwera*.

ine

ine, literally "me," would normally be indicated as a pronominal suffix *-nga* to the preceding genitive marker *pa*, the equivalent of the Hebrew preposition ל when used with personal pronouns (e.g. לי for "my"), as in *panga*.

iemwe

See Laws' use of *emwe*, verse 4, for a slightly different but equally incorrect vocalization of the "who," *yemwe*, in the attributive comparative ο ισχυροτερος. The attributive nature of this construction is better indicated as the prefix *wo-* in the *wopambana*, where *pambana* is the word for "surpassing" that follows. It needs specification of the area in which he "surpasses" him (John the Baptist). Laws has this *wopambana* in his translation and it makes the *iemwe* redundant.

ali

Ali, "is," is an effort at indicating the stative (as opposed to transitive) nature of the attributive comparative. However, this element is also a part of the prefix *wo-* in *wopambana* and is therefore redundant.

wampamvu

The repetition of the properties in *wo-* indicated in the *wa-* of *wamphavu* (notice Laws' omission of *h* in his vocalization) makes for awkward syntax. The appropriate possibilities are ***wamphamvu kupambana ine*** or ***wopambana ine mphamvu***. Further, *kupambana ine* can be reduced to *kundipambana* and *wopambana ine* can be reduced to *wondipambana* by incorporating μου into the comparative infix as *-ndi-*. This leaves the options ***wamphamvu kundipambana*** and ***wondipambana mphamvu***.

dzikwatakwata

This far this represents the first effort at translating the concept in the noun. *Dzikwatakwata* takes the sound of walking in sandals, *kwata-kwata*, the equivalent of English "flip-flop," and makes it into a noun by adding the plural/dual prefix *dzi-*. *Buku Lopatulika* abandoned this rather very innovative term for *nsapato* and *Buku Loyera* followed suit. I would argue, though, that *dzikwatakwata* is more graphic and closer to the sandal of New Testament times in the holy land, than the nondescript *nsapato* (shoes) that hardly anyone uses to refer to sandals in the Chewa or Nyanja speaking areas of central Africa.

dzatshi

In verse 3 Laws had *zatshi* for the same work. His struggle in hearing *tsh* where he should be hearing *ch* or *c* continue here. We find another area of challenge with the phonology of the language: *dz* or *z*. *Buku Lopatulika* rendered this *zace*.

woenera
Read *woyenera*. In addition, *sindiri woyenera* is collapsible to *sindiyenera* in a construction that recognizes that first person stative verb "I am" in *wo-* is already present in the *-ndi-* of the preceding word.

weramira
Since *ku weramira* is an aorist participle modifying the infinitive *ku masula*, the insertion of the conjunction *ndi*, "and" is the appropriate way to interpret the construction: *kuweram[ir]a* **ndi** *kumasula*, "to stoop down and untie." See the translations adopted in the KJV, NIV and NAS.

Verse 8

Dinabapatiza inu ndi madzi; koma ie adzabapatiza inu ndi Nzimu Woyera.

Dinabapatiza
There being no Nyanja equivalent for βαπτιζω, "baptize," the options include adopting a Nyanja transliteration that is vocalized like the Greek, hence *bapati[d]za*, or a paraphrase. Laws chose the first option. Yet, the prefix *dina-* does not convey the subject and tense/aspect of the aorist active indicative first person singular. This requires either **ndina-** or the gnomic (the essence of his continuing activity) aorist **ndi-**. In addition, *ndinabapatiza/ndibapatiza inu* is collapsible to *ndinakubapatizani/ndikubapatizani* by incorporating the accusative plural object pronoun, υμας, *inu*, in the verb as the infix *-ku-* and suffix *-ni*.

ie
Should read *iye*.

adzabapatiza
adza-bapatiza inu is a correct rendering of the future tense or contingency. However, as above, *adzabapatiza inu* is collapsible to *adza-**ku**-bapatiza-**ni***.

Nzimu
Laws' faulty vocalization *Nzimu* actually exists in the cognate Nsenga dialect as the noun for "bees." The Nyanja (Western Nyanja or Chewa dialect) for "Spirit" is *Mzimu* with an *m* not an *n*.

B.i.b. Commentary Summary

This brief analysis and commentary has revealed the following. Laws' grasp of Nyanja phonology, morphology and syntax is very elementary and often flawed. Indications of this include the following: failure to discern how verb-roots change with different tense aspects;[10] failure to adequately translate prepositions[11] and case functions;[12] failure to translate connectives properly;[13] failure to understand the intricate system of prefixes, infixes and suffixes and how these replace independent relative, subject and object pronouns.[14] When he seems to understand the general concepts, he does not always use the correct affixes.[15]

It also reveals that Laws' knowledge of Nyanja etymology, and therefore his ability to translate dynamically, is very poor.[16] His vocabulary is equally very limited.[17] His Nyanja phonology is misleading at several points.[18] He has not grasped the syllabification and vocalization of Nyanja.[19] The vast majority, if not all of the above are errors that deep and sustained interaction with the Mang'anja would have easily corrected.

Laws was apparently aware of this fact but judged the task to be too demanding for his European epistemological constitution: "It takes much time and patience, also close contact with the natives, to grasp the true idiom of a language. Even with the greatest effort, diligence and perseverance, it seems almost impossible for a European to get at the real inner meaning of the native mind."[20]

We may therefore conclude that, in translating the Scriptures and related material into Nyanja, Laws was quite aware of the inadequacies of his work and was motivated to do so for purely pragmatic reasons in the absence of better alternatives. It is hardly surprising, therefore, that, when the decision

---

10. *alembedwa* (v. 2), *adzakonzetsa* (v. 2), *emwe anabapatiza* (v. 4) etc.
11. *m'Yesaya* (v. 2).
12. *la modzi* (v. 3), *la kutembenuza* (v. 4), *kwa kubweza* (v. 4), *ali wampamvu* (v. 7) etc.
13. *ndimo* (v. 5), *alinkudza* (v. 7), *dinabapatiza* (v. 8) etc.
14. *emwe* (v. 4), *omwe* (v. 5), *iemwe* (v. 7), *dinabapatiza* (v. 8).
15. *naturuka* (v. 5).
16. For examples see *invangeli* (v. 2), *mprofeti* (v. 2) and *mbapatisma* (v. 4).
17. See *fotokoza* (v. 3), *mwini* (v. 3) and *nauza* (v. 4).
18. See *invangeli* (v. 1), *nthenga, nkope* (v. 2), *m'tshipululu, zatshi* (v. 3), *zimpulupulu* (v. 5), *m'ntsinje* (v. 5), *gamila, tshikopa, m'tshunu, utshi, muntengo* (v. 6), *pambuiu* (v. 7), *nzimu* (v. 8) etc.
19. See *kuamba* (v. 1), *emwe* (v. 4), *ie* (v. 5), *ubwea* (v. 6) and *woenera* (v. 7).
20. Laws, *Reminiscences of Livingstonia*, 127–28.

was made to find a translation that could be suitable for use by all missions, Laws' New Testament was found to be "a poor translation."[21]

NYANJA REVISION PANEL, 1925.
Left to Right—Dr. W. H. MURRAY (Dutch Reformed Church); Dr. HETHERWICK (Church of Scotland); Dr. LAWS (U.F. Church of Scotland); and Rev. D. G. MALAN (Dutch Reformed Church).
Dr. Laws was the first to translate any part of the Bible into the Nyanja language, completing St. Mark's Gospel in Western Nyanja in 1880.

Figure 5. The Union Nyanja Revision Panel. 1925. Left to Right – Dr. W. H. Murray (Dutch Reformed Church); Dr. Hetherwick (Church of Scotland); Dr. Laws (U. F. Church of Scotland); and Rev. D. G. Malan (Dutch Reformed Church).[22]

---

21. Retief, *William Murray of Nyasaland*, 96.

22. Image in: W. C. Somerville, *From Iona to Dunblane: The Story of the National Bible Society of Scotland to 1948* (Edinburgh: The National Bible Society of Scotland, 1948), 49. Used by permission.

12

Laws' Translation of Mark 1:1–8 in the Light of Scott's[1] and the Union Nyanja[2] Translations

To facilitate immediate comparison, Scott's translation[3] and the Union Nyanja translation[4] have been juxtaposed with Laws' translation. The actual commentary and comparison is to be found immediately below each verse.

Comparative Commentary
Verse 1

Laws	Scott	Union Nyanja
Kuamba kwa invangeli wa Yesu Kristu, Mwana wa Mulungu.	KUYAMBA KWA MTENGA-WA-BWINO WA IESU KIRISTU.	CHIYAMBI chache cha Uthenga Wabwino wa Yesu Kristu, Mwana wa Mulungu.

Scott has recognized the titular nature of verse 1, hence the capitalization. His vocalization of Nyanja syllables is more enlightened than Laws' but also erratic: *kuyamba* is correctly vocalized with a *y*, but *mtenga* does not bear the spirant *th*. In addition, his transliterations, *Iesu* and *Kiristu*, are either

---

1. *Mtenga-wa-Bwino wa Iesu Kiristu Mbuye watu ndi Mpulumutsi* (Edinburgh: The National Bible Society of Scotland, 1893).
2. *Buku Lopatulika ndilo Mau a Mulungu: Chipangano cha Kale ndi cha Tsopano* (Edinburgh: National Bible Society of Scotland and British and Foreign Bible Society, 1922).
3. This is indicated as the second level in each verse.
4. This is indicated as the third level in each verse.

not in Bantu syllables (*Iesu* where *Yesu* should stand) or awkwardly done (*Kiristu* where *Kristu* should stand). The prefix *ku-* in *kuyamba* is infinitival and inappropriate for an impersonal noun where *chi-* should stand. However, he is already showing greater familiarity with Nyanja idiom in translating ευαγγελιου *mtenga* although he does so inaccurately. The correct prefix should be *u* as in *uthenga* because *mthenga* means "messenger."

The Union Nyanja demonstrates great strides forward on several fronts. It bears none of the vocalization and grammatical problems noted above. By capitalizing all the nouns in the verse, it too has noted the titular nature of this verse in Nyanja narrative. Perhaps its only shortcoming is the transliteration of Christ as *Kristu*, omitting an *h* after *K*. This error has been corrected in the *Buku Loyera* of 1998.

Verse 2

Laws	Scott	Union Nyanja
Inde monga alembedwa m'Yesaya, mprofeti	Monga mwa lembedwa m'Hesaia mlaula yo,	Monga mwalembedwa m'Yesaya mneneri,
Ona dituma ntenga wanga patsogolo pa nkope yako;	Onani ! ndi tuma wamtenga wanga patsogolo pako,	Ona, ndituma mthenga wanga patsogolo pa nkhope yanu,
Emwe adzakonzetsa njira yako;	Amene adzapanga njira yako,	Amene adzakonza njira yanu;

Scott's translation does not include the inexplicable *Inde*. He has made a great effort to indicate that εν τω Ησαια τω προφντη is an implicit reference to a book or scroll by adopting the locative prefix *m-* in *mwa*, "it [is] in," with *Hesaia* and with *laula*, the last noun intensified by the suffix *yo*. This gallant effort is, however, subject to misunderstanding. He would have done better by translating the locative fully using the impersonal *chi-na-* or *cha-* prefix for the reality of "being" (perfect tense) written. An example would be *monga chi-na-lembedwa mwa-mneneri Yesaya*. Scott's transliteration, *'Hesaia*, does not follow Bantu phonology. However, he yet again tries to translate προφητη although his word of choice, *laula*, literally "utter a taboo," is misleading.

The Union Nyanja is not much further on. They adopt Scott's effort at translating the locative by prefixing *m-* before *lembedwa* and *Yesaya*, though their transliteration follows Bantu phonology. Their choice of noun to translate προφητη is, however, well-researched: *nenera* is a root that is appropriate for the Hebrew נבא, literally "speak under the influence of a spirit," "in an ecstatic state," etc.[5] The repetitive, inspired or ecstatic nature of the speaking or prophesying is reflected in the reduplication of a root that would otherwise be *nena*, "speak." The prefix *m*- and suffix ending -*i* makes a noun of this root, *mneneri*, the equivalent of the attributive participle "one who prophesies."

Verse 3

Laws	Scott	Union Nyanja
Liu la modzi kulira m'tshipululu,	Mau a wo pfuula m'chipululu!	Mau a wopfuula m'chipululu,
Fotokozani njira ya mwini,	Konzani kwalala la Mbuye	Konzani khwalala la Ambuye,
Pangani njira zatshi zolungama;	Lungamitsani njira zache.	Lungamitsani njira zache;

Here we have a clear demonstration of the difference between Scott and Laws' grasp of Nyanja. Scott uses the collective singular *mau* for singular φωνη, captures both the singular subject and the genitive case in the attributive participle βοωντος using the prefixes *a-wo-*, "of one who," uses the correct noun *pfuula* for "crying out" or "proclaiming" and writes the word for "wilderness," *chipululu*, correctly. The Union Nyanja cannot improve on this at all.

In the following clause, Scott's only error is not making *k* in *kwalala* aspirant, a matter that the Union Nyanja does by adding an *h* after *k*. However, in this particular case, Laws' *njira* is a better choice than the improvised *khwalala*. *Konzani*, not Laws' *fotokozani*, correctly stands for Ετοιμασατε. Likewise, *Mbuye*, not Laws' *mwini* stands for κυριος. *Mbuye* and *Ambuye* are interchangeable and purely a stylistic matter.

In the second imperatival clause, Scott has correctly understood the relationships in the two object accusatives to their verb and has translated ευθειας ποιειτε using one verb, *lungamitsa*.

Yet again, the Union Nyanja cannot improve on this.

---

5. BDB, 612.

Verse 4

Laws	Scott	Union Nyanja
Yohane nadza, emwe anabapatiza m'tshipululu Nauza	Pa na to kala IOANNE na-tsira-antu-madzi m'chipululu ! nalalakira	Yohane anadza nabatiza m'chipululu, nalalikira
mbapatisma la kutembenuza ntima kwa kubweza kwa zimpulupulu.	chitsiridwe cha madzi cha ku-tembenuka-mtima kwa kuchosa michimwo.	ubatizo wa kutembunuka mtima wakuloza ku chikhululukiro cha machimo.

In *Pa na to kala*, read *khala*, Scott is demonstrating his knowledge of the genre of Nyanja story-telling, probably learned as he listened to the Mang'anja tell didactic tales to the young around fireplaces. The construction, particularly in the Chewa dialect of Mang'anja, is indeed normative for the introduction of narrative prose, as frequent as Hebrew ויהי, "and it happened that/it was," in Hebrew narrative prose. Further, Εγενετο is the overwhelming choice for translating the Hebrew ויהי in the LXX. For examples see Genesis 27:1; Exodus 12:51; 16:27; Joshua 1:1; Judges 1:1etc. However, the context seems to favour the nuance "come" for γινομαι, with Ιωαννης as its subject, leading to *anadza*, "he came." Scott transliterates Ιωαννης into English and not Nyanja as Laws and the Union Nyanja committee do. Moreover, unlike both Laws and the Union Nyanja committee, he translates [ὁ] βαπτιζων using the word *tsira*, "sprinkle" or "smear," to which he adds the noun *madzi*, "water," and the direct object *antu* (read *anthu*) "people." This may represent his Christian tradition's practice in administering the rite of baptism and hence a theological interpretation. His choice for translating κηρυσσων, *lalikira*, is well researched and adopted by the Union Nyanja. Contrast this with Laws' choice (*nauza*). Finally, in translating the participles [ὁ] βαπτιζων and κηρυσσων predicately, Scott and the Union Nyanja have implicitly decided to translate εγενετο with the nuance "came" and modified by the predicate participles. This makes Scott's *pa na to kala* even less convincing.

Scott is consistent with his use of *tsira* in *chitsiridwe cha madzi*, "sprinkling of water." However, in translating μετανοιας with the suffix *-ka* (as opposed to Law's *-za*), he has understood it as a genitive of description/attributive genitive. All three translations have attempted a dynamic (meaning-based) translation at this point by supplying the noun *mtima*, "heart," της καρδιας, to μετανοιας. Scott has *kuchosa*, "removal," where Laws had *kubweza* ("returning") for αφεσιν. But the Union Nyanja has improved on both by adopting *wakuloza* *ku chikhululukiro*, "leading to forgiveness." The common noun for "sin" or the better understood "transgression" is the Nyanja *chimo*. Laws' *mphulupulu* is an acceptable synonym. However, Scott's version of the plural, *michimwo* is inexplicable where *machimo*, as the Union Nyanja has it, should stand. Perhaps he is trying to create a noun from the verb *kuchimwa* ("to sin") by prefixing *mi* to the root *chimw-* and adding the suffix *o*.

Verse 5

Laws	Scott	Union Nyanja
Ndimo naturuka kwa ie dziko lonse la Yudeya, ndi onse omwe a Yerusalem;	Ndipo pa na li ku turuka ku dza pa iye dziko lonse la Ioudaia ndi a Ierusalemu onse,	Ndipo anaturuka a ku dziko lonse la Yudeya, ndi a ku Yerusalemu onse;
ndimo nabapatizidwa ndi ie m'ntsinje Yordan,	na-li-ku-tsiridwa-madzi naye m'mtsinje wa Iordana	nadza kwa iye nabatizidwa ndi iye mu m'tsinje Yordano,
kubvumbula zimpulupulu zao.	ndi kubvomerezera michimwo yao.	poulula machimo awo.

Scott's rendering of the simple subject+verb construction, και εξεπορευετο ... πασα η Ιουδαια Χωρα και Ιεροσολυμιται as *ndipo pa na li ku turuka ... dziko lonse la Ioudaia ndi a Ierusalemu onse*, "and there was a coming out ... the whole countryside of Judah and all the inhabitants of Jerusalem," is quite unwarranted where the simpler and correct *anaturuka*, "they came out" (if the people are the immediate subject), or *linaturuka*, "it came out" (if *dziko*, "the countryside" as a metaphor for the people is the immediate subject) should stand. Other weaknesses include his transliteration of the proper names; translation of προς αυτον as *pa iye* ("at him") instead of *kwa iye*, "to him"; and failure to capture the locative idea inherent in the noun οι Ιεροσολυμιται by inserting the prefix *m-* before it. The Union Nyanja is better and more consistent. However, its use of *ku* for the locative idea in *Yerusalemu* is inappropriate where *mu-* should stand if the inhabitants of the city of Jerusalem are intended.

Scott's *na-li-kutsiridwa-madzi naye* literally reads "[and] were being sprinkled/smeared [with] water with/by him." But *naye* is Nsenga not Chewa *ndi iye* for "by/with him." The Union Nyanja has fully captured the idea of εξπορευετο by complementing *anaturuka* "they came out" with *nadza* "[and] came." Scott did this by inserting *ku-dza* in his unorthodox translation. In contrast, Laws only has *naturuka*. Scott's form of the locative prefix *mu-* before the noun *mtsinje*, "river," lacks the vowel. Finally none of the translations has transliterated Ιορδανη properly where perhaps *Yordane* or *Yordani*[6] should stand.

Where Laws had *kubvumbula*, "uncovering" or "disclosing," Scott has *kubvomerezera*, an attempt at translating as "agreeing with" and the Union Nyanja has *poulula*, "upon disclosing" for εξομολογουμενοι. However, as pointed out in the earlier comment with respect to Laws' effort, none of these choices adequately incorporates the element of culpability. *Lapila* is a better choice than all of them.[7] We have already noted Scott's problem with the plural form of *chimo*.

Verse 6

Laws	Scott	Union Nyanja
Ndimo Yohane wabvala ndi ubwea wa gamila, nali ndi	Ndipo Ioanne a nali wobvala ubwea wa ngamira ndi	Ndipo Yohane anabvala ubwea wa ngamila, ndi
lamba la tshikopa m'tshunu mwatshi, ndimo nadia madzombe ndi utshi wa muntengo.	lamba la chikopa pa chuunu chache, ndi wodya maomba ndi uchi wa m'tengo.	lamba la chikopa m'chuuno mwache, nadya dzombe ndi uchi wa ku thengo.

Scott has correctly rendered the perfect participle ενδεδυμενος with the prefix *a nali-* in *a nali wobvala*. But the Union Nyanja's *anabvala* is even better because it has collapsed *anali-* and *wo-* in *ana-*. None of the translations has vocalized *ubweya* correctly.[8] Union Nyanja's *Ngamila* and not Scott's *ngamira* is the noun "camel."

Like Laws, Scott and Union Nyanja have *la* as the indicator of the attributive accusative δερματινην. Scott is hearing *chuunu* while Union Nyanja has *chuuno* for *chiuno*[9] for "waist." Both Scott and Union Nyanja have *chikopa* where Laws heard **tshikopa**. Scott's *maomba* must be an obscure synonym for *dzombe* and is correctly discarded by Union Nyanja. Union Nyanja correctly understood *dzombe* to be a collective now, where Laws had felt the need for an extra plural

---

6. *Buku Loyera* has *Yordani*.

7. *Buku Loyera* continues with *kuulula*, "disclosing," which lacks the unstated "repenting" element in the Greek εξομολογουμενοι as used here.

8. As *Buku Loyera* eventually did.

9. Or *chiwuno* as *Buku Loyera* has it.

marker in **madozmbe**. Finally, Scott is still failing to read the spirant form in *mtengo*, corrected to *thengo* in the Union Nyanja version.

Verse 7

Laws	Scott	Union Nyanja
Ndimo nauza, kuti, Alinkudza pambuiu pa ine	Ndipo a na lalikira ndi ku ti, Wo ndi pambana ine mpamvu a li ku dza pambuyo panga,	Ndipo analalikira, kuti, Wondipambana ine mphamvu akudza pambuyo panga,
iemwe ali wampamvu wopambana ine, zingwe za dzikwatakwata dzatshi sindiri woenera ku weramira ku masula.	wa amene ine si ndi enera ku weramira ndi ku masulira alamba a nsapato zache.	sindiyenera kuweramira kumasula lamba la nsapato zache.

Scott's *a na lalikira **ndi** kuti* is a departure from his own confession about the halo of the narrative tense. That would have demanded *analalikira nati*. Further, the *ine* in *wo ndipambana ine* is an unnecessary repetition of the first person pronoun already present in *wondipamba* as the infix *-ndi-*. This error is perpetuated in the Union Nyanja. Also notice Scott's faulty vocalization of *mpamvu* corrected in the Union Nyanja rendering *mphanvu*.

Scott's *wa* in *wa amene* is redundant as *ou-* is already represented in *amene*. Laws and the Union Nyanja have not translated this relative pronoun. Notice also how Scott has correctly connected κυψας λυσαι with the conjunction *ndi* (and) where Laws and the union Nyanja have maintained the literal but wooden and confusing *kuweramira kumasula* "stooping untying."

In another rare reversal, Laws' *zingwe za dzikwatakwata* is better syntax than Scott's *alamba a nsapato zache* (because *lamba* can be a collective plural noun) and Union Nyanja's *lamba la nsapato zache* (because the fact that *lamba* is plural demands that the *la* be the plural *za*). Further, in his choice of *zingwe*, "strings," over *lamba*, "belt," Laws has chosen the superior word equivalent for the Greek ιμαντα.[10]

---

10. *Buku Loyera* vindicates Laws' choice by adopting *zingwe*.

Verse 8

Laws	Scott	Union Nyanja
Dinabapatiza inu ndi madzi; koma ie adzabapatiza inu ndi Nzimu Woyera.	Ine ndi-na-tsira-inu-madzi, koma uyu a-dza-ku-tsirani-inu ku Mzimu-wo-yera.	Ndakubatizani inu ndi madzi; koma Iye adzakubatizani ndi Mzimu Woyera.

Scott's *ine* at the beginning recognizes the emphatic nature of the pronoun εγω, a feature that is absent from both Laws' translation and the Union Nyanja. His choice of *tsira* becomes even more problematic here because, with the dative υδατι, "in/with water," water is specifically mentioned and he dare not repeat it. However, Laws and the Union Nyanja apparently share Scott's theological interpretation of βαπτιζω in that their preference for rendering the dative instrumentally, namely *ndi*, "with," lends itself more to the idea of sprinkling[11] than the locative *mu*, "in," which suggests immersion.

All three translations have tried to translate the second emphatic αυτος: Laws as *ie*, Scott as *uyu*, "this one," and Union Nyanja as *iye*. Yet in *a-dza-ku-tsirani-inu*, Scott has a redundant *-inu* since the third person plural object pronoun is already present in the verb as the suffix *-ni*.

Comparative Commentary Summary

The superiority of Scott's grasp of Nyanja phonology, grammar, syntax, vocabulary, and idiom over that of Laws is evident at several points. He had a keen understanding of Bantu phonology and concomitant vocalization.[12] His vocabulary was broader[13] and this helped him to attempt dynamic equivalence translation more often than Laws.[14] However, he did not vocalize proper nouns using principles of Bantu phonology and vocalization.[15] He had a keen

---

11. As also the *Buku Loyera* has it. To be fair, several English versions, including the NET, NIV, ESV, GNT, NLT and RSV, translate this dative using "with." However, the ברית חדשה, the New Testament translation of the Greek New Testament into Modern Hebrew, has במים, clearly favouring the idea of "in water" than "with water" which would have required עם מים.

12. See *Kuyamba, ndi tuma* (v. 2), *m'chipululu* (v. 3), *Ierusalemu, m'tsinje* (v. 5) and *pambuyo* (v. 7). Also see his comment in Scott, *A Cyclopaedic Dictionary*, viii, under the heading "PHONOLOGY": "Bantu syllables are always open – i.e., they always end in a vowel."

13. For examples see *mtenga* (v. 1), *mlaula, pfuula, kwalala, Mbuye, lungamitsani* (v. 3), *tsira* (v. 4), *maomba*.

14. See the examples in the note above.

15. For examples see the half attempt in *Kiristu* (v. 1), and the transliterations *Hesaia* (v. 2), *Ioanne* (v. 4), *Ioudaia, Ierusalemu, Iordana* (v. 5).

understanding of the complex system of Bantu affixes and how they impacted grammar:

> Mang'anja, like other Bantu tongues, is called a prefix language; but the prefixes are not so much initial syllables as modulations of the first letters of the noun, the echo of these modulations being caught up by the attributes of the noun and by its verb. When we come to consider the making of verbs and nouns, we find that suffix changes are also used to express various modifications of the original root meaning; other particles are grouped after the prefix and before the verb to express tense modifications, and the prefixes are set free to connect noun with attribute or noun with verb.[16]

Finally, he demonstrates a superior knowledge of Nyanja etymology and idiom.[17]

However, this superiority was not without its blemishes. Scott failed at several points to hear the spirant.[18] There is the occasional failure to vocalize Nyanja words correctly.[19] There is the problem of transliterating proper nouns without sensitivity to Bantu phonology.[20] There is the occasional failure to use the correct affix.[21] Finally, there is the occasional poor word choice.[22]

The Union Nyanja betrays its indebtedness to Scott's translation at several points. Several of his word choices are adopted.[23] This indebtedness includes adopting Scott's errors.[24] At times, their departure from Scott's translation compromised quality.[25]

---

16. See *mwa lembedwa, ndi tuma, adzapanga* (v. 2), *a wo pfuula, lungamitsani* (v. 3), *na-tsira-antu-madzi . . . na lalikira* (v. 4), *wo ndipambana, alikudza . . . panga* (v. 7), etc. Scott, *A Cyclopaedic Dictionary*, x.

17. For examples, see *mtenga-wa-bwino* for ευαγγελιου (v. 1), *Onani!* for Ἰδου, itself a translation of the Hebrew הנה (Exod 23:20 *BHS*) (v. 2), *pfuula, kwalala, Ambuye* for κυριος, *lungamitsani, pa na to kala, tsira* (v. 4), *turuka . . . ku dza*, as a translation of the one verb εξπορευετο, *kubvomerezera* (v. 5), *lalikira, kuweramira* **ndi** *kumasulira* (v. 7).

18. See *mtenga* (v. 1), *kwalala* (v. 3), *kala* (v. 4), *m'tengo* (v. 6) and *mpamvu* (v. 7).

19. See *ubwea, ngamira* (v. 6) and *enera* (v. 7).

20. See *Iesu* (v. 1), *Hesaia* (v. 6), *IOANNE* (v. 4), *Ioudaia* (v. 5), etc.

21. See *mtenga* (v. 1), *Onani! . . . pako* (v. 2), *michimwo* (vv. 4 and 5) and *chuunu* (v. 6).

22. See *mlaula, adzapanga* (v. 2), *kwalala* (v. 3) and *alamba* (v. 7).

23. For examples see *Uthenga wa Bwino* (v. 1), *monga mwa lembedwa, Amene* (v. 2), *mau a wopfuula* (v. 3), *khwalala la Ambuye* (v. 3), *lungamitsani njira* (v. 3), *nalalikira* (v. 4), *wondipambana ine mphavu . . . pambuyo panga* (v. 7), etc.

24. See *monga mwalembedwa m'Yesaya* (v. 2), *khwalala* (v. 3) and *ubwea* (v. 6).

25. Compare Scott's *turuka . . . kudza* with their *turuka* (v. 5) and Scott's *weramira ndi ku masulira* (v. 7) with their *kuweramira kumasula* (v. 7).

However, there are points where the Union Nyanja has improved on Scott's translation. They have vocalized proper nouns using Bantu syllables.[26] They have picked up on the spirant forms.[27] At points they have made better word choices.[28] They have also improved on word forms.[29]

From the above, it is quite evident that, in spite of Retief's claim that Scott's translations of the four Gospels were not suitable for use by other missions,[30] Scott's translation of Mark 1:1–8 is the document behind the Union Nyanja translation of 1922 while Laws' translation scarcely features in it. Indeed, the findings of Murray, the man commissioned by the Union Nyanja Translation committee to prepare the original draft of the New Testament for consideration by the committee, upon consulting with Hetherwick at Blantyre, seems to negate this observation. He noted that:

> In the course of this revision, remarkably little difference was found between the Blantyre and Mvera grammatical forms, and yet it was sometimes difficult to find the right word which would satisfy both parties. There had of course to be a mutual give and take sometimes and then the form against which the least could be said was chosen. The revisers themselves were occasionally not quite satisfied with the result but it was the best they could do, and anyway it meant a great deal that a translation was evolved which satisfied both parties.[31]

The Immediate Impact of Laws' Translations in Central Africa

Evangelism was the primary motive for Laws' pragmatic approach to the reduction of Mang'anja to writing: "When the native language had been sufficiently acquired, the evangelistic work developed rapidly. Truths about God, the future life, and daily duty were constantly unfolded, and the dark citadel of heathenism was powerfully attacked."[32] This fact comes up often whenever Laws gave an account of the work at Livingstonia. Several of these

---

26. See *kristu* (v. 1), *Yesaya* (v. 2), *Yohane* (v. 4), *Yudeya* and *Yerusalemu* (v. 5).

27. See *uthenga* (v. 1), *mthenga* (v. 2), *khwalala* (v. 3) and *mphamvu* (v. 7).

28. See *m'neneri* (v. 2), *adzakonza* (v. 2), *nabatiza* (v. 4) and *chikhululukiro* (v. 4).

29. See *mum'tsinje, machimo* (v. 5) and *ngamila* (v. 6).

30. Retief, *William Murray of Nyasaland*, 96.

31. Retief, *William Murray of Nyasaland*, 98.

32. J. W. Jack. *The Story of the Livingstonia Mission British Central Africa* (Edinburgh and London: Oliphant, Anderson & Ferrier, 1901), 1115.

accounts were before the National Bible Society of Scotland who played a major role in funding, facilitating and printing Bible translations for Central Africa.[33]

One such account suggests that Africans were so endeared by these translations that they were willing not only to pay for the cost of their publication, but also to contribute towards carriage expenses:

> The natives have paid the cost of all that have been published. The carriage out to Lake Nyassa is a very serious item of expense, but now they are meeting part of that also. You will find our teachers in Ngoni-land working for three months and giving the whole of their wages that they may have a New Testament or Bible of their own; and the people all through our mission stations are anxious to have these Gospels and willing to pay for them.[34]

To Laws, this degree of eagerness for the Scriptures represented the true measure of the progress of mission and commerce:

> If you want to know about the progress of civilisation throughout the world, in all that is really worthy of the name civilisation and that has respect to the good of the people in this world or in the world to come, you can get no better index than the work of the Bible Society and the circulation of the Scriptures throughout the world.[35]

The fact that these accounts predate the translations of the Bible by the fidelity-conscious Union Nyanja Bible Translation Committee means that the Scriptures in question are the eclectic translations undertaken by whosoever dared to translate. These translations inspired and fueled mission in its infancy. The Union Nyanja was proposed in order to address two issues. First, to meet the need for a translation of the Bible into the Nyanja language that would be acceptable to all the missions using that language. Second, to enhance translation fidelity by involving a team of translators as opposed to the many single-translator texts that were already in use. The initial meeting was convened at Fort Johnston in May 1900.[36]

---

33. For an example, see *Quarterly Record* (July 1905): 189–90, a publication of the Bible Society of Scotland. Also see Appendix VII, Laws' personal letter to D. Knight of the National Bible Society of Scotland.

34. Rev. Robert Laws, M.D.D.D. AGM of the Society held 26 February, 1900 at which Laws was present, *Quarterly Record* (April 1900): 637.

35. *Quarterly Record* (April 1900): 636.

36. Hetherwick, *The Romance of Blantyre*, 120.

However, this underscores the earlier observation that the popularity of a translation does not necessarily correspond to its quality. From this perspective, it is quite clear that Laws' translations, as the Union Nyanja after them, were widely accepted by the readership and stood as the inspired Word of God for their generation. It is a mark of the stature of the Union Nyanja translation that nearly a century later, it is still in great demand: "Some 106 years after the appearance of Dr Laws' first Gospel, the Glasgow printing firm William Collins are about to undertake on behalf of the Bible Society, a reprint of over 70,000 copies of the Bible in this language."[37]

---

37. Binnington, "Where Have All The Bibles Gone?"

Part IV

Going Forward

13

Consequences of Developments Since the Twentieth Century

Bible Translation Practices

Several developments have happened in the field of Bible translation since the days of Hugh Goldie of Old Calabar (modern Nigeria), D. C. Scott of Blantyre and Robert Laws of Livingstonia (modern Malawi). Disparate Bible translation agencies organized and coalesced into focused and efficient organizations.

Scottish Presbyterians would today be sent by or at least seconded to the Scottish Bible Society in Edinburgh, or their sister British and Foreign Bible Society located in Swindon, England. They would be part of the global fellowship called the United Bible Societies whose membership currently exceeds 150 countries. All the translators would be mother-tongue speakers, assisted by experts in biblical studies and linguistics. If they are translators in Anglophone and Francophone Africa,[1] they would undergo basic training in the source languages: biblical Hebrew and biblical Greek. Their training would also include translation theory and practice, the OT and NT in their cultural settings, OT interpretation and hermeneutics, linguistics and translation, and discourse analysis of OT and NT texts. In addition, some of them would have spent about a month in Israel, acquainting themselves with the geography and history of the holy land.

Primarily, these developments are intended to ensure that mother-tongue speakers, preferably members of the ethnic groups into whose languages the

---

1. The United Bible Societies is present in four regions, formerly hubs: Africa, Americas, Europe and Asia. Translators in each region are trained by United Bible Societies certified Bible Translation Consultants (and other personnel) in curricula developed regionally in keeping with the needs of each region. Anglophone Africa and Francophone Africa have developed a customized curriculum for training Bible translators in Africa.

Bible is being translated, are the translators in a project. They are also intended to acquaint the translator with developments in translation theories since Bible translation began, leading to informed choices about how each Bible translation project is to proceed in its task. They are intended, as much as possible, to reduce distortions and misrepresentations of source texts particularly through eliminating the need to translate from translations. Finally, the developments are intended to make the communities for whom the Bible is being translated the key players and owners of the process of translation.

Both the translators and target communities would be trained by a team of Bible Translation Consultants who are experts in biblical studies, linguistics and translation studies to various degrees. Several of them would be indigenous to the continent of Africa and mother-tongue speakers of the Bible translation projects and languages that they are supervizing and working with as lead consultants. Within United Bible Societies, these standards and practices are replicated in all the four regions.

Several other Bible translation organizations are now part of the global effort to translate the Bible into all the languages of the world. These organizations are collaborating at several levels to ensure maximum benefit from scarce resources, and a basic quality of translations. Such collaboration occurs at several levels and under several initiatives, including the Forum for Bible Agencies International (FOBAI).

All the above means that Bible translation in Africa today must be weighted in favour of the agency of Africans. However, the "elephant in the room" is the low level of competence in knowledge of the source texts and their backgrounds: the languages themselves, the histories, geographies and social-cultural realities of the communities to whom the texts belong. The more competence in these fields of knowledge is attained by translators and other supporting personnel in the translation process, the better translation-as-interpretation Africans will produce. As has been noted, even in everyday communication praxes, communication depends on "speaker and hearer sharing the same competence."[2] That is to say, capacity building in all these areas is Africa's biggest challenge if epistemological hegemony from other parts of the world is to be overcome.

The current scenario is still weighted in favour of the agency of non-Africans, or at least provision of their critical support in this "re-telling" activity. Even in the United Bible Societies, there are still several Bible translation

---

2. M. Davies, "Postructural Analysis," in D. N. Freedman, ed., *The Anchor Yale Bible Dictionary*, vol. 5 (New York: Doubleday, 1992), 424.

projects where the consultant is not from the continent of Africa. In addition, even where the consultant is African, he or she is working with several projects outside their linguistic, geographical, historical and social-cultural comfort zones. In other words, each African consultant is only working with a handful of translation projects where they can claim to have mother-tongue or near-mother-tongue competence. This unhappy scenario means that the critical task of interpreting the source texts is still largely in the hands of "foreigners."

Without building capacity, even the re-evaluations that the oral/aural nature of the source texts brings, and the expansion of translation theories to revolve around the comprehensive centre of need to communicate, will not take off from the ground. The epistemological hegemony of foreigners, including African foreigners, will continue. One translation organization, the United Bible Societies, has understood this challenge, even if perhaps for other reasons.[3] A robust program to develop translation consultants in each of its member countries is currently underway.

Linguistics

There have also been significant developments in the understanding of languages since the nineteenth century. Hughes and Laws were working with so-called universal principles of grammar. At the time, languages were understood as being essentially the same, only differing in complexity on a perceived evolutionary scale. Some African languages, for example, were perceived to be still quite underdeveloped and incapable of communicating some concepts. Study of all languages had involved historical and etymological deconstructive analysis intended to understand language through its development (evolution), in the light of categories identified in perceived more evolved languages. However, Ferdinand de Saussure's (1857–1913) structuralism came to dominate linguistics as time went on, advocating for the study of language as a system (*langue*) from which the meanings of specific utterances (*parole*) can be understood. This made the *synchronic* study of a language more important than the traditional *diachronic* study.[4] This thinking was applied, in various ways, "to almost all the sciences and the humanities; in every case" trying "to show that meaning and significance result from the way human beings pattern

---

3. For example, the realization that home-grown expertise is cheaper, in the long run, than flying experts into different countries.
4. F. de Saussure, *Course in General Linguistics* (New York: McGraw Hill, 1974), 7–17.

their intellectual systems."[5] Structuralism demanded competency in *langue*, the whole structure, before one can understand *parole*, specific creations within the structure. Originality that transcended the structure was viewed as an illusion.[6] Rather, languages and literatures ought to be treated as autonomous from the world around them and examined using their internal structures.[7]

In biblical studies, James Barr's *The Semantics of Biblical Language*[8] proved to be a decisive turn in moving the discipline to embrace structuralism. Preoccupation with philological studies focusing on the diachronic study of languages[9] gave way to studies seeking to derive meanings of individual texts (*parole*) from perceived structures of the entire corpus (*langue*). Meaning was the function of contextual use within a text, not some supposed meaning derived from diachronic studies. For this reason, structuralism has led to close attention to the rhetorical organization of biblical texts in literary criticism: "The arrangement of elements within the text is thus taken as highly significant, and much attention is devoted to the shaping of texts through repetitions, chiastic arrangement, and stereotyped formulas, as well as by contrasting pairs (binary opposition)."[10]

The problem for religious texts is that structuralism abandons the search for authorial intentions (critical in communication) "and acknowledges a text's multiplicity of possible meanings."[11] Although the concerns of structuralism are valid, the word of God is supposed to be obeyed, not rendered incoherent in terms of its specific prescriptions and demands. A bigger problem is the fact that communication is the glue of human relations, and goes on, although shared *competence* between speaker and hearer is problematic. This is reflected in Derrida's *différance*,[12] "which both expresses the insights of structuralism, that meaning is relational rather the essential, and conveys the further insight that meaning is indefinitely deferred, never completely captured and defined

---

5. J. Barton, "Structuralism," in D. N. Freedman (ed.), *The Anchor Yale Bible Dictionary*, vol. 6 (New York: Doubleday, 1992), 214.

6. Barton, "Structuralism," 215.

7. Davies, "Postructural Analysis," 424.

8. James Barr, *The Semantics of Biblical Language* (Oxford, 1961).

9. See as an example the iconic work, G. Kittel and G. Friedrich, eds., *Theological Dictionary of the New Testament*, 10 vols, trans., G. W. Bromley (Grand Rapids: Eerdmans, 1964–76).

10. Barton, "Structuralism," 216.

11. Davies, "Postructural Analysis," 425.

12. J. Derrida, *Dissemination*, trans. B. Johnson (London, 1981).

by an utterance."[13] Even in biblical studies, despite pretensions to the contrary, exegesis can only access so much of the original communication:

> Pragmatists have been content to accept that language is useful in affording communication within social systems, without searching for a metalanguage which would allow escape from this relativist position. Such a stance involves a conservative attitude toward the institutions which give language its sense and significance. In biblical studies, too, we cannot always be unaware of cultural and institutional influences on religious language, even when presented in the form of commentaries on the Bible. Commentaries from the Middle Ages seem alien in their interests and concepts to people living in the 20th century, but even commentaries written by contemporaries in English betray their sectarian bias.[14]

This resonates with the theory of translation as communicating the message in source texts into target texts in biblical translation. It also resonates with the complexity of this transfer of meaning that has made concepts like "equivalence" no longer tenable, opening to the door instead to concepts like "loyalty" in Christiane Nord's Skopos theory, "similarity," and the like. It validates the breadth of such theories as complexity theory. Finally, it resonates with the critical nature of shared competence between "speaker and hearer," source text and translator (and other stakeholders in the translation process). It is *competence* in the two spheres that will protect the message of the source texts from unacceptable distortions in the target texts.

Poststructuralist linguistics has opened the door to the study of each language on its own terms, leading to radical revisions of the nature of language in its different manifestations. Structuralist grammatical analyses have given way to descriptive grammatical analyses and freed languages from being examined through imposed lenses. Research has revealed that all languages are complex and have equal capacity to communicate any concept adequately and competently.

Bible translation in Africa must leverage this new space by making descriptive analyses of target languages, preferably by mother-tongue linguists, part of the process of translation. In many instances, such expertise is not immediately available to translation teams and must be deliberately sought out. This could take the form of engaging relevant institutions that are involved

---

13. Davies, "Postructural Analysis," 425.
14. Davies, "Postructural Analysis," 425.

in such analyses of vernacular languages in government institutions and/or institutions of higher education. For example, when the author was working with the Shona Study Bible[15] in Zimbabwe, a Shona expert at the University of Zimbabwe's African Languages and Research Institute (ALRI)[16] was brought into the project to guide the Shona translators and reviewers in the orthography (particularly reducing phonemes to writing), syntax and semantics of the Shona language.

Translation Theories

As a human activity, translation goes back into antiquity and employed various approaches, including within the same corpus. For example, the particulars of the process of translating the Septuagint are shrouded in hazy, often contradictory traditions.[17] It is possible, however, to imagine some of this process, albeit imprecisely, by retrospectively considering the corpus: "Examination of the text . . . indicates a combination of numerous versions both literal and free and marked by considerable variance in style, interpretation of the Hebrew, and even order and contents; the latter suggests a variety of underlying Hebrew texts."[18] Similarly, in the Graeco-Roman world, translation was already an official practice that could either be literal, word for word (in legal and government documents) or free, to the point of the translation differing markedly from the original.[19]

In the first chapter, we discussed the evolution of translation theories in Bible translation to the present. Ongoing developments are enhancing the conversation of translation as communication and increasing the agency of

---

15. *Bhaibheri Rechishona Rine Tsanangudzo* (Harare: The Bible Society of Zimbabwe, 2020).

16. Dr. Matambirofa, the expert in question, is a Shona and his field of study is the Shona language. At the time, he was the Director of ALRI. According to its official website, the ALRI is "an inter-disciplinary, semi-autonomous and non-faculty research unit at the UZ [University of Zimbabwe] dedicated to the research, documentation and development of African indigenous languages in Zimbabwe. Its research agenda focuses mainly on corpus development and maintenance, computational lexicography and language technology applications." Its mission is "To research, document and develop Zimbabwean indigenous languages in order to promote and expand their use in all spheres of life." https://www.uz.ac.zw/index.php/departments-arts/293-alri, accessed on 25 September, 2022.

17. H. B. Swete, *An Introduction to the Old Testament in Greek* (Cambridge: Cambridge University Press, 1914), 6–26.

18. A. C. Myers, *The Eerdmans Bible Dictionary*, Rev. Ed. (Grand Rapids: Eerdmans, 1987), 154.

19. P. A. Noss, *A History of Bible Translation* (Rome: Edizioni Di Storia E Letteratura, 2007), 13.

target audiences in the task of Bible translation. Marais' complexity theory is one such development. Central to this theory is recognition that many influences are involved in the communication process, without diminishing the value of any.[20] It is the antithesis of reductionism, without diminishing the value of reductionism itself from the understanding of communication.[21]

However, theories applied in actual translation practice tend to lag behind cutting edge scholarly developments. For example, as noted above, current practice in the United Bible Societies still tends to be the pursuit of meaning-based translations with little thought given to what is *actually* going on in terms of fidelity to the source texts. In the minds of the average translation practitioner, theories such as "equivalence," "re-telling," "similarity," or "loyalty," to name a few, are not in conscious thought as they work. That is for the scholar trying to describe what is going on. The translators are just trying to do their best in mediating the message of the source texts into their target text. And, in this matter, the premium is on the capacity/competence to understand or hear the message of the source texts and to communicate it faithfully into the target text.

Ongoing Challenges

All the developments highlighted above demonstrate the critical nature of the consideration of the question "Whose epistemology is at play in the Bible translation process?" Interaction of languages in the translation process, the transfer of meaning from one language to another, demands clarity on this question. This is because it is possible to be aware of all the developments above, and still short-change the target communities by imposing foreign epistemologies upon them by the way their Bibles are translated.

It is not enough that Bible translators today are mother-tongue speakers and indigenous people. The power relationships in a Bible translation project between translator, consultant and community are such that the voice of the consultant may prevail and override those of the other two. Where such a consultant is foreign to the target community, this reverts to foreign epistemological hegemony. Further, it is also acknowledged in several sources that even indigenous consultants and translators can be operating under the

---

20. K. Marais, *Translation Theory and Development Studies: A Complexity Theory Approach* (London: Routledge, 2014), 19.

21. K. Marais, "Complexity in Translation Studies," in Yves Gambier & Luc van Doorslaer, eds., *Handbook of Translation Studies*, vol. 5 (Amsterdam: John Benjamins, 2021), 24.

influence of foreign epistemologies due to their education, training and similar contacts with other epistemologies.

African scholars during and following the political independence of African societies from their colonial masters have argued successfully that, to paraphrase the language of one of them, the colonization of the African mind has remained even where political power has passed into African hands. This is the logical consequence of over half a century of negative profiling and suppression of African cultural practices, ways of thinking and languages by the colonial classes, often portrayed as part of the necessary transformation from heathenism to Christianity. In some cases, even African names, so full of cultural and epistemological capital, were discarded and replaced by European names. The net results of all this are huge chunks of Africans who despise or, at the very least, are very suspicious of their own ontologies, including languages and epistemological foundations.

Adversely, it is possible for mother-tongue speakers and communities to drown the voice of the other interlocutor, the source text, in their quest for naturalness and clarity. The target community are not the originators of the communication that is being negotiated and they ignore the complexity and packaging of the source texts at their own peril.

Suggestions Going Forward

It is important for Africans to understand, as Lamin Sanneh's studies around the subject of the translatability of Christianity forcefully argue, that Christianity transcends and transforms the different cultures that it encounters. Its *modus operandi* is to enter each successive culture and to transform it from within. It does not obliterate cultures.

In addition, developments in linguistics and translation theory have opened mighty doors for African agency in translating the Bible into their languages. From the philological studies that preceded structuralism, through the reductionistic tendencies and negative perceptions of African languages (and cultures) in modernity, to post-structuralist studies, Africans can minimize the distortions in their vernacular Bibles through attaining competence in source language texts and their own languages. They have the opportunity to "re-tell" the word of God to their communities directly from Hebrew, Aramaic and New Testament Greek texts.

This calls for deliberately using the epistemological tools found in each society and culture, for harvesting what resonates with source language realities and cultures, working around the realities that are very different, and producing

Bible translations that transfer meanings from the source languages into target languages using the materials that are at present found in the latter. At the end of this process, the African must feel that the God of the Bible speaks to them in their languages.[22] When meaning and communication take centre stage, faithful transfer of the message of the Bible has a chance.

For many African communities, Bible translation is a critical part of the translatability of Christianity into their societies. As such, starting with the very process of translation (whether textual, oral, using sign language or other forms of media), the message of the Bible must incarnate into the languages and communities that it encounters. The following suggestion will help this process.

1. The training of the translators and consultants must include, at the project level, deliberate consideration and incorporation of the philosophy of the target language in comparison with the philosophies of the source languages. Consideration of epistemology must be at the centre of these considerations. Involving a target language linguist in a translation project is a good first step, where such expertise is not present at a high level among the translators and the consultant.

2. Where the translators will depend on other translations, due to lack of adequate competence in the source languages, such training should include consideration of the philosophies of those languages as well. They must understand very well that they are taking the scenic route and must be privy to the added challenges of such a route.

3. The communities that will be involved in the process of translation, especially the community reviewers, must also be made aware of the dynamics of the philosophies of language that are at play at the various levels of translation.

4. The translation community in Africa should continue to move towards acquiring adequate competence, at all levels, in both the source texts and the target texts.

---

22. A. O. Mojola, *God Speaks My Language* (Carlisle, UK: Hippo Books, 2020).

Conclusion

In Part I, we established that the Enlightenment, a European phenomenon, was very influential in the formation of nineteenth-century epistemology for Europeans. We also established that this epistemology was an extension of the Hellenic-European phase of epistemological dominion. Finally, we established that, although the Modern Missionary Movement predated the expansion of imperialism, the two agendas shared a common epistemological constitution and views of civilization.

In Parts II and III, we established that the Scottish Presbyterian missionaries to Old Calabar and Central Africa came with the same epistemological theory and practice, one that bore the imprint of the Enlightenment. In language theory, this entailed a scientific approach to reducing the vernacular languages to writing and translation – albeit one that was not always, as in the case of Goldie of Old Calabar and Scott of Blantyre Mission, overtly intended. We have also established that well-articulated and developed theories of translation were not a feature of the massive translation exercises undertaken during the nineteenth century by the protagonists of mission in Old Calabar and Central Africa.

We found the Efik New Testament to have been a work of great industry and done by a man who was extraordinarily conscious of both his functional superiority over the Calabarese and his epistemological distance from Africans. Yet, there was no African contribution in matters of text and exegesis. This was the case because Africans lacked the expertise to engage these issues, but also because they were not expected to contribute at that level.

We found the circumstances of the Nyanja translation of Mark to be similar to those of the Efik New Testament with the caveat that Laws was probably not conscious of his functional superiority over the Mang'anja and his epistemological distance from Africans to the same degree that Goldie was. An analysis of Laws' translation of Mark 1:1–8 demonstrates how his epistemological distance and the exclusion of Africans in the critical aspects of his translation drastically compromised its quality. Yet, its wide acceptability demonstrates how his status and authority as a Scottish missionary translated into high regard for his work.

The critical examination of the two projects has, therefore, suggested[23] and demonstrated[24] that they were undertaken under the circumstances

---

23. This is in reference to the Efik New Testament whose analysis did not involve a specific text.

24. This is in reference to Laws' translation of Mark 1:1–8.

of epistemological exclusivism with respect to critical African agency and participation, and epistemological hegemony with respect to European missionary participation. The quality of subsequent Bible translation work could only improve on these aberrations by involving the critical participation of Africans at the levels of text and exegesis, of understanding vernacular languages within the translation team and the level of translation into the vernacular.

In Part IV, we revisited the developments that have taken place in translation practices and agency, linguistics and translation theories. We have noted the ongoing challenges and made suggestions, going forward, for the realization of African agency in vernacular Bible translation and the attainment of competence in source language texts and target texts.

Appendix I

The New American Standard and Greek New Testament texts of Mark 1:1–8

New American Standard[1]

Mark 1:1-8

¹The beginning of the gospel of Jesus Christ, the Son of God.
   ²As it is written in Isaiah the prophet,

      "Behold, I send My messenger before Your face,
         Who will prepare Your way;
   ³"The voice of one crying in the wilderness,
      'Make ready the way of the Lord,
         Make His paths straight.'"

⁴John the Baptist appeared in the wilderness preaching a baptism of repentance for the forgiveness of sins. ⁵And all the country of Judea was going out to him, and all the people of Jerusalem; and they were being baptized by him in the Jordan River, confessing their sins. ⁶And John was clothed with camel's hair and *wore* a leather belt around his waist, and his diet was locusts and wild honey. ⁷And he was preaching, and saying, "After me One is coming who is mightier than I, and I am not fit to stoop down and untie the thong of His sandals. ⁸"I baptized you with water; but He will baptize you with the Holy Spirit."

---

1. *Holy Bible. New American Standard* (Nashville, TN: Broadman & Holman Publishers, 1977).

Greek New Testament[2]

Mark 1:1-8

¹ἈΑρχὴ τοῦ εὐαγγελίου Ἰησοῦ Χριστοῦ [υἱοῦ θεοῦ].
²Καθὼς γέγραπται ἐν τῷ Ἠσαΐᾳ τῷ προφήτῃ,

> Ἰδοὺ ἀποστέλλω τὸν ἄγγελόν μου πρὸ προσώπου σου,
> ὃς κατασκευάσει τὴν ὁδόν σου·[3]
> ³φωνὴ βοῶντος ἐν τῇ ἐρήμῳ,
> Ἑτοιμάσατε τὴν ὁδὸν κυρίου,
> εὐθείας ποιεῖτε τὰς τρίβους αὐτοῦ[4]

⁴ἐγένετο Ἰωάννης [ὁ] βαπτίζων ἐν τῇ ἐρήμῳ καὶ κηρύσσων βάπτισμα μετανοίας εἰς ἄφεσιν ἁμαρτιῶν. ⁵καὶ ἐξεπορεύετο πρὸς αὐτὸν πᾶσα ἡ Ἰουδαία χώρα καὶ οἱ Ἱεροσολυμῖται πάντες, καὶ ἐβαπτίζοντο ὑπ' αὐτοῦ ἐν τῷ Ἰορδάνῃ ποταμῷ ἐξομολογούμενοι τὰς ἁμαρτίας αὐτῶν. ⁶καὶ ἦν ὁ Ἰωάννης ἐνδεδυμένος τρίχας καμήλου καὶ ζώνην δερματίνην περὶ τὴν ὀσφὺν αὐτοῦ, καὶ ἐσθίων ἀκρίδας καὶ μέλι ἄγριον. ⁷καὶ ἐκήρυσσεν λέγων, "Ἔρχεται ὁ ἰσχυρότερός μου ὀπίσω μου, οὗ οὐκ εἰμὶ ἱκανὸς κύψας λῦσαι τὸν ἱμάντα τῶν ὑποδημάτων αὐτοῦ· ⁸ἐγὼ ἐβάπτισα ὑμᾶς ὕδατι, αὐτὸς δὲ βαπτίσει ὑμᾶς ἐν πνεύματι ἁγίῳ."

---

2. *The Greek New Testament*, edited by Kurt Aland, et al., Third Edition (Corrected) (Stuttgart: United Bible Societies, 1983).

3. ιδου οδον σου Exod 23:20; Mal 3:1.

4. φωνη αυτου Isa 40:3.

Appendix II

Sample text of Laws' working translation of the Gospel of Mark, 1885[1]

---

1. *Ivangeli wa Marko*, Handwritten copy of Working Draft. National Bible Society of Scotland, Edinburgh. Robert Laws. Used by Permission.

Appendix III

A copy of the letter of Robert Laws to the Rev. D. Knight, NBSS, 1928[1]

> Rev. D. Knight
> National Bible Society of Scotland
> 5 St Andrew Square, Edinburgh.
>
> 69 Merchiston Crescent,
> Edinburgh, Feb. 29, 1928.
>
> Dear Dr Knight,
>
> I am sorry not to be present at the Annual Meeting of the N.B.S. in Glasgow that I might have the opportunity of telling something of what the assistance your Society rendered to the workers in Central Africa, has done for the Christianization of the country.
>
> In 1878, when I went out first there was not a single school or church in all that vast region, & the task of reducing the languages of the people to writing lay before the workers. Now in Nyasaland in addition to the work of the Universities & other Missions, the presbyteries of the Livingstonia Blantyre & Dutch Reformed Church Missions have formed a Synod, with more than 50,000 church members & a still greater number of Catechumens & adherents. With your help the Scriptures have been put into their hands. The first 6,700 N.Tests. of the Union Version in Nyanja, weighing 4½ tons sent out in 1912 have been followed by repeated consignments of the whole bible, & portions of it, printed in that language, numbering up till now over 100,000 copies, & the demand is still unexhausted.
>
> The N.Test. in whole or in part has been printed in several other languages as well, & it is in the help given to these smaller tribes who cannot face, unaided, the cost of printing & transport of such scriptures that the help you have given us is so specially valuable. All this means that God's word is in growing measure taking its place in the hearts & homes of these peoples who 50 years ago were living in darkness & fear, but now are seeking to mould their lives & conduct according to the example of our Lord Jesus Christ.
>
> This work has been made possible by the help of the Bible Societies, and if I want to know how Christianity & Civilization are advancing in the world, the most reliable information I can find is the circulation of the scriptures as shown in their annual reports.
>
> With all my heart I thank you for the help you have given my fellow workers & myself in past years, and I pray that still greater prosperity may be yours in the service of our Lord in this particular department of His work, in the years to come.
>
> With kind regards, Yours Sincerely,
> Robert Laws

---

1. Edinburgh University Library Special Collections. *Laws' Collection*, Gen. 562.

Bibliography

Primary Sources
A. Archives
EUL Edinburgh University Library Special Collections
Papers of Robert Laws, Coll-75, Gen. 562, University of Edinburgh
Scott's Collection, Gen. 717/10.
Waddell, entry for Tuesday 4 Dec. 1849, Journals, vol. VII.
Waddell, entry for 19 Feb. 1850, Journals, vol. VII.

NBSS National Bible Society of Scotland, Edinburgh
Robert Laws. *Ivangeli wa Marko*. Handwritten copy of Working Draft.
———. *Ivangeli wa Mwini Watu Ndi Mpulumutsi Yesu Kristu kwa Marko*. Edinburgh: Printed for the National Bible Society of Scotland, 24 April 1885. First Proofs.
———. *Maivangeli a Mwini Watu Ndi Mpulumutsi Yesu Kristu Kwa Mateyu, Marko, Luka, ndi Yohane*. Edinburgh: Printed for the National Bible Society of Scotland, 1885. Final Handwritten Copy and Printed Proofs.
———. *Testamente Watsopano wa Mwini Watu Ndi Mpulumutsi Yesu Kristu. Mau a Tshinyanja*. Edinburgh: Printed for the National Bible Society of Scotland, 19 February 1885. First Proofs; 28 May 1885. Second Proofs.

NLS National Library of Scotland, Edinburgh
Blantyre, 7876, 7876/151
Cape Maclear, 7909
Kaning'ina, 7910
Law's Diary, 7907
Livingstonia, 7876/244, 7912, 8021

B. Periodicals
Christian Express, June 1880, September 1886.
Life and Work in British Central Africa, April and June 1895.
Quarterly Record, April 1900 and July 1905.
The Central African Planter, Vol. 1. No. 8, April 1896.
The Commission, July 1858.
U.P. Missionary Record, 1850.

Secondary Sources
A. Published Books

Ajayi, J. F. A. *Christian Missions in Nigeria, 1841–1891: The Making of a New Élite.* London: Longmans, Green and Co. Ltd., 1965.

Ashcroft, B., Gareth Griffiths and Helen Tifin. *Key Concepts in Post-Colonial Studies.* London and New York: Routledge, 1998.

Bailey, R. C., and T. Pippen, eds. "Race, Class and the Politics of Biblical Translation." *Semeia* 76. Atlanta: Scholars Press, 1996.

Balden, S. K. "The Politics of Modern Russian Biblical Translation." *Bible Translation and the Spread of the Church: The Last 200 Years.* Edited by Philip C. Stine. Leiden: E. J. Brill, 1990.

Bar-Efrat, S. *Narrative Art in the Bible*, 2nd ed. Bible and Literature Series 8. Sheffield: Academic Press, 1984.

Barton, J. "Structuralism." In D. N. Freedman, ed. *The Anchor Yale Bible Dictionary.* Vol. 6. New York: Doubleday, 1992.

Beekman, J., and J. Callow. *Translating the Word of God.* Grand Rapids: Zondervan Publishing House, 1974.

Bhaibheri Rechishona Rine Tsanangudzo. Harare: The Bible Society of Zimbabwe, 2020.

Booth, J. *Africa for the Africans.* Edited by Laura Perry. Blantyre, Malawi: CLAIM, 1996.

Buku Lopatulika ndilo Mau a Mulungu: Chipangano cha Kale ndi cha Tsopano. Translated by the Union Nyanja Translation Committee. Edinburgh: National Bible Society of Scotland and British and Foreign Bible Society, 1922.

Buxton, T. F. *The African Slave Trade and Its Remedy.* London, 1840.

Cairns, H. A. C. *Prelude to Imperialism: British Reaction to Central African Society 1840–1890.* London: Routledge & Kegan Paul, 1965.

Coldham, G. E., comp. *African Scriptures.* Vol. 1. *A Bibliography of Scriptures in African Languages.* London: The British and Foreign Bible Society, 1966.

Comaroff, J., and J. Comaroff. *Of Revelation and Revolution.* Vol. 1. *Christianity, Colonialism, and Consciousness in South Africa.* Chicago: University of Chicago Press, 1991.

Cust, R. N. *A Sketch of the Modern Languages of Africa: Accompanied by a Language Map.* Vol. I. London: Trubner, 1883.

Dana, H. E., and J. R. Mantey. *A Manual Grammar of the Greek New Testament.* Toronto, Ontario: Macmillan, 1957.

Davies, M. "Postructural Analysis." In D. N. Freedman, ed. *The Anchor Yale Bible Dictionary.* Vol. 5. Doubleday, 1992.

Derrida, J. *Dissemination.* Trans. B. Johnson. London, 1981.

De Ward, J., and E. A. Nida. *From one Language to Another: Functional Equivalence in Bible Translating.* Nashville: Thomas Nelson, 1986.

Dickie, W. *Story of the Mission in Old Calabar.* Mission of the United Presbyterian Church. Edinburgh: Offices of the United Presbyterian Church, 1894.

Dickson, K. A. *Uncompleted Mission: Christianity and Exclusivism*. Maryknoll: Orbis Books, 1991.

Dike, K. O. *Trade and Politics in the Niger Delta*. Oxford: Oxford University Press, 1956.

Drummond, H. *Tropical Africa*. London: Hodder & Stoughton, 1888.

Dyrness, W. A. *Learning about Theology from the Third World*. Grand Rapids: Zondervan Publishing House, 1990.

East Central Africa, Livingstonia: The Mission to Lake Nyassa, 2nd ed. Edinburgh: Free Church, 1876.

Forde, D., ed. *Efik Traders of Old Calabar*. Oxford: Oxford University Press, 1957.

Gadamer, H. *Truth and Method*. London: Sheed and Ward, 1975.

Gitari, D. M., and G. P. Benson, eds. *Witnessing to the Living God in Contemporary Africa*. Nairobi: African Theological Fraternity, 1986.

Goldie, H. *Calabar and its Mission: with additional chapters by Rev. John Taylor Dean*. Edinburgh and London: Oliphant, Anderson & Ferrier, 1901.

———. *Memoir of King Eyo VII of Old Calabar: A Christian King in Africa*. Old Calabar: United Presbyterian Mission Press, 1894.

———. *Principles of Efik Grammar: with Specimen of the Language*. Edinburgh: Muir and Paterson, 1868.

Greenberg, M. *Introduction to Hebrew*. Englewood Cliffs: Prentice-Hall, Inc., 1964.

Grimley, J. B., and G. E. Robinson. *Church Growth in Central and Southern Nigeria*. Grand Rapids: Eerdmans Publishing House, 1966.

Hammond, P. B., ed. *Cultural and Social Anthropology: Selected Readings*. New York: The Macmillan Company, 1964.

Hastings, A. *A History of African Christianity 1850–1975*. Cambridge: Cambridge University Press, 1976.

Hetherwick, A. *The Romance of Blantyre: How Livingstone's Dream Came True*. London: Clarke & Company, Ltd., 1931.

Historical Catalogue of the Printed Editions of Holy Scripture in the Library of the British and Foreign Bible Society. Vol. II. 1. *Polyglots and Languages Other than English*. Compiled by T. H. Darlow and H. F. Moule. London, 1903; reprint New York: Kraus Reprint Corporation, 1963.

Holmes, J. S. *Translated! Papers on Literary Translation and Translation Studies*. Amsterdam: Rodopi, 1988.

Jack, J. W. *The Story of the Livingstonia Mission British Central Africa*. Edinburgh and London: Oliphant, Anderson & Ferrier, 1901.

Johnson, B. ed. *Freedom and Interpretation*. Oxford Amnesty Lectures. New York: Basic Books, 1993.

Johnston, H. *The Backward Peoples and Our Relations with Them*. London, New York, Melbourne, Cape Town, Bombay, Calcutta, Madras, Shanghai, Peking, Copenhagen: Oxford University Press, 1920.

Jones, G. I. *Trading States of the Oil Rivers*. Oxford: Oxford University Press, 1963.

Knight, W. *The Missionary Secretariat of Henry Venn*. London, 1882.

Larson, M. L. *Meaning-Based Translation: A Guide to Cross-Language Equivalence*. Lanham: University of America, 1984.

Laws, R. *Reminiscences of Livingstonia*. Edinburgh: Oliver and Boyd, 1934.

Lepsius, R. *Standard Alphabet for Reducing Unwritten Languages and Foreign Graphic Systems to a Uniform Orthography in European Letters*, 2nd ed. London: Williams Norgate, 1863.

Linden, I. "The Maseko Ngoni at Domwe, 1870–1900." *Early History of Malawi*. Edited by B. Pachai. London: Longamans, 1972.

Livingstone, D. *Dr. Livingstone's Cambridge Lectures: Together with a Prefatory Letter by the Rev. Professor Sedgewick*. Cambridge: Deighton, Bell, 1858.

Livingstone, W. P. *A Prince of Missionaries: Alexander Hetherwick*. London: James Clarke, 1931.

———. *Laws of Livingstonia*. London: Hodder & Stoughton, 1921.

Luzbetak, L. J. *The Church and Cultures: New Perspectives in Missiological Anthropology*. Maryknoll: Orbis Books, 1988.

Macdonald, D. *Africana: or the Heart of Heathen Africa*. Vol. 2. Edinburgh: John Menzies, 1882.

Machen, J. G. *New Testament Greek for Beginners*. Englewood Cliffs: Prentice Hall, 1923.

Marais, K. "Complexity in Translation Studies." In Yves Gambier & Luc van Doorslaer, eds. *Handbook of Translation Studies*. Vol. 5. Amsterdam: John Benjamins, 2021.

———. *Translation Theory and Development Studies: A Complexity Theory Approach*. London: Routledge, 2014.

Maxey, J. A. *From Orality to Orality: A New Paradigm for Contextual Translation of the Bible*. Eugene: Cascade Books, 2009.

Mbiti, J. S. *New Testament Eschatology in an African Background*. London: Oxford University Press, 1971.

———. *The Prayers of African Religion*. Maryknoll: Orbis Books, 1975.

———. *The Study of African Religion & Philosophy*. London: Heinemann, 1969.

McCracken, K. J. *Politics and Christianity in Malawi: 1875–1940*. Cambridge: Cambridge University Press, 1977.

McFarlan, D. M. *Calabar, the Church of Scotland Mission, 1846–1946*. Edinburgh, 1946.

McIntosh, H. *Robert Laws: Servant of Africa*. The Stables, Carberry, Scotland: The Handsel Press Ltd., 1993.

McKerrow, J. *History of the Foreign Missions of the Secession and United Presbyterian Church*. Edinburgh: Andrew Elliot, 1867.

Mead, M. *Growing Up in New Guinea*. New York: Mentor Books, 1953.

Mojola, A. O. *God Speaks My Language*. Carlisle, UK: HippoBooks, 2020.

Morrison, J. H. *Streams in the Desert: A Picture of Life in Livingstonia*. London: Doran, 1919.

Mtenga-wa-Bwino wa Iesu Kiristu Mbuye watu ndi Mpulumutsi. Translated by D. C. Scott. Edinburgh: The National Bible Society of Scotland, 1893.

Mufuka, K. N. *Missions and Politics in Malawi*. Kingston, Ontario: The Limestone Press, 1977.

Mugambi, J. N. K. *From Liberation to Reconstruction: African Christian Theology After the Cold War*. Nairobi, Kenya: East African Educational Publishers Ltd., 1995.

Myers, A. C. *The Eerdmans Bible Dictionary*. Rev. Ed. Grand Rapids: Eerdmans, 1987.

Neill, S. C. *A History of Christian Missions*. Harmondsworth: Penguin, 1964.

Newbigin, L. *Foolishness to the Greeks: The Gospel and Western Culture*. Geneva: World Council of Churches; Grand Rapids: Eerdmans, 1986.

Newmark, Peter. *A Textbook of Translation*. New York: Prentice Hall, 1988.

Nida, E. A., ed. *The Book of a Thousand Tongues*, rev. ed. London: United Bible Societies, 1972.

Nida, E. A., and C. A. Taber. *Theory and Practice of Translation*. Brill Academic Publishers, 2003.

Nomenyo, S. "Theology in the Life of the Churches." *African Challenge*. Edited by Kenneth Y. Best. Nairobi, Kenya: Transafrica Publishers, 1975.

Nord, C. "Functionalist Approaches." In Y. Gambier & L. Van Doorslaer (eds), *Handbook of Translation Studies*. Vol. 1. Amsterdam/Philadelphia: John Benjamins, 2010.

North, E. M. "Eugene A. Nida: An appreciation." *Language, Culture and Religion: in Honour of Eugene A. Nida*. Edited by Matthew Black and William A. Smalley. The Hague: Mouton, 1974.

Noss, P. A. *A History of Bible Translation*. Rome: Edizioni Di Storia E Letteratura, 2007.

———. "Current Trends in Scripture Translation." In P. A. Noss, ed. *Current Trends in Scripture Translation*. Bulletin Number 194/195. Reading, UK: United Bible Societies, 2002.

Obufa Testament: *Abon Ye Andinyana Myin Jisus Krist*. Translated by Goldie Hugh. Edinburgh: Murray Ye Gibb, 1862.

Oliver, R. *Sir Harry Johnston and the Scramble for Africa*. London: Chatto and Windus, 1957.

———. *The Missionary Factor in East Africa*. London: Longman, 1952; rep. 1970.

Pachai, B., ed. *Livingstone, Man of Africa, Memorial Essays 1873–1973*. London, 1973.

———. *Malawi: The History of the Nation*. London: Longman, 1973.

Parrinder, G. *West African Religion*. London, 1949.

Retief, M. W. *William Murray of Nyasaland*. Translated by Mary H. Le Roux and M. M. Oberholster-Le Roux. Cape Town: The Lovedale Press, 1958.

Rhoads, D. "What is Performance Criticism?" In H. E. Hearon and P. Ruge-Jones (eds), *The Bible in Ancient and Modern Media: Story and Performance*. Eugene: Cascade Books, 2009.

Robinson, R., and J. Gallagher. *Africa and the Victorians: the Official Mind of Imperialism*. London: Macmillan, 1961.

Ross, A. C. *Blantyre Mission and the Making of Modern Malawi*. Blantyre, Malawi: CLAIM, 1996.

Ross, K. R., ed. *Christianity in Malawi: A Source Book*. Gweru, Zimbabwe: Mambo Press, 1996.

Sanneh, L. *Encountering the West. Christianity and the Global Cultural Process: The African Dimension*. London: Marshall Pickering, 1993.

——— *Translating the Message: The Missionary Impact on Culture*. Maryknoll: Orbis Books, 1989.

Saussure, F. de. *Course in General Linguistics*. New York, 1974.

Schleiermacher, F. D. E. *Hermeneutics: The Handwritten Manuscripts*. Edited by H. Kimmerle. Missoula: Scholars Press, 1977.

Schon, J. F., and S. Crowther. *Journals of the Expedition of 1841*. C. M. S. 1842.

Scott, D. C. *A Cyclopaedic Dictionary of the Mang'anja Language spoken in British Central Africa*. Edinburgh: The Foreign Missions Committee for the Church of Scotland, 1862.

Seow, C. L. *A Grammar for Biblical Hebrew*, rev ed. Nashville: Abingdon Press, 1995.

Sidhom, S. "The Theological Estimate of Man." *Biblical Revelation and African Beliefs*. Edited by K. A. Dickson and P. Ellingworth. London: Lutterworth Press, 1969.

Sindima, H. J. *The Legacy of Scottish Missionaries in Malawi*. Studies in the History of Missions, Volume 8. Lampeter, Wales: The Edwin Mellen Press, 1992.

Smalley, W. A. *Translation as Mission: Bible Translation in the Modern Missionary Movement*. The Modern Mission Era, 1792–1992: An Appraisal. Macon: Mercer University Press, 1991.

Somerville, W. C. *From Iona to Dumblane: The Story of the National Bible Society of Scotland to 1948*. Edinburgh: The National Bible Society of Scotland, 1948.

Southon, A. E. *Gold Coast Methodism*. London: Cargate Press, 1934.

Stewart, J. *Livingstonia: its Origins*. Edinburgh: Andrew Elliot, 1894.

Sugirtharajah, R. S. *Postcolonial Criticism and Biblical Interpretation*. Oxford: Oxford University Press, 2002.

Swete, H. B. *An Introduction to the Old Testament in Greek*. Cambridge: Cambridge University Press, 1914.

Tarr, D. *Double Image: Biblical Insights from African Parables*. New York and Mahwah: Paulist Press, 1984.

Taylor, J. V. *The Growth of the Church in Buganda*. London: S.C.M. Press, 1958.

Testamente Watsopano wa Mwini Watu ndi Mpulumutsi Yesu Kristu: Mau a Tshinyanja. Translated by Robert Laws. Edinburgh: Printed for the National Bible Society of Scotland, 1886.

The Complete Works of John Wesley. Vol. XI. London, 1872.

The Nigeria Catholic Directory. 7 Simisola Road, Sure-Lere, P.M.P., Yaba, Nigeria: National Office, 1962.

Thiong'o, N. Wa. *Decolonising the Mind: The Politics of Language in African Literature*. London: James Currey Ltd., 1986.

Thiselton, A. C. *New Horizons in Hermeneutics: The Theory and Practice of Transforming Biblical Reading*. London and New York: HarperCollins, 1992.

Thomas, T. R. H. *Narrative of the Expedition to the River Niger in 1841*. 2 vols. London, 1848.

Thompson, J., ed. *From Nyassa to Tanganyika: The Journal of James Stewart CE in Central Africa 1876–1879*. Blantyre, Malawi: Central Africana, 1989.

——— *Touching the Heart: Xhosa Missionaries to Malawi, 1876–1888*. African Initiatives in Christian Mission 5. Pretoria: University of South Africa, 2000.

Vaughan C., and V. E. Gideon. *A Greek Grammar of the New Testament*. Nashville: Broadman Press, 1979.

Venuti, L. *Translation Changes Everything: Theory and Practice*. Abingdon, Oxon: Routledge, 2013.

Vries, L. De. "Local Oral-Written Interfaces and the Nature, Transmission, Performance, and Translation of Biblical Texts." In J. A. Maxey and E. R. Wendland (eds.), *Translating Scripture for Performance: New Directions in Biblical Studies*. Eugene: Cascade Books, 2012.

Waddell, H. M. *A Vocabulary of the Efik or Old Calabar Language: With Prayers and Lessons*. Edinburgh: Grant and Taylor, 1849.

———. *Twenty-Nine Years in the West Indies and Central Africa: a Review of Missionary Work and Adventure 1829–1858*, 2nd ed. Missionary Researches and Travels No. 11. London: Frank Cass and Company Limited, 1870.

Walls, A. F. "Samuel Ajayi Crowther 1807–1891: Foremost African Christian of the Nineteenth Century." *Mission Legacies: Biographical Studies of Leaders of the Modern Missionary Movement*. Maryknoll: Orbis Books, 1994.

Wa Thiong'o, N. *Decolonising the Mind: The Politics of Language in African Literature*. London: James Currey Ltd., 1986.

———. *Homecoming: Essays on African and Caribbean Literature, Culture and Politics*. London: Heinemann, 1972.

Welbourn, F. B., and B. A. Ogot. *A Place to Feel at Home: A Story of Two Independent Churches in Western Kenya*. London: Oxford University Press, 1966.

Wells, J. *Stewart of Lovedale*. London: Hodder & Stoughton, 1908.

Wendland, E. E. *The Cultural Factor in Bible Translation: A Study of Communicating the Word of God in a Central African Cultural Context*. UBS Monograph Series, No. 2. London, New York, Stuttgart: United Bible Societies, 1987.

West, G. O. *Biblical Hermeneutics of Liberation*, 2nd rev. ed. Maryknoll: Orbis Books, 1995.

Wittgenstein, L. *Philosophical Investigations*. Oxford: Blackwell, 1967.

Young, E. D. *Mission to Nyassa, a Journal of Adventures*. London: Longmans, 1877.

Young, R. F. *Resistant Hinduism: Sanskrit Sources on Anti-Christian Apologetics in Early 19th Century India*. Nobili Research Library 8. Vienna: Institut für Ideologie der Universität Wien, 1981.

B. Journals

Forster, P. G. "Missionaries and Anthropology: The Case of the Scots of Northern Malawi." *Journal of Religion in Africa* 16. No. 2 (1986): 101–120.

Gallagher, J. "Fowell Buxton and the New African Policy." *Cambridge Historical Journal* 11 (1950).

Hermanson, E. A. "A brief overview of Bible translation in South Africa." *Acta Theologica Supplementum* 2. 22 (1) (2002): 6–18.

Makutoane, et al. "Similarity and alterity in translating the orality of the Old Testament in oral cultures." *Translation Studies* 8 (2) (2015): 156–174.

Naudé, J. A. "From Submissiveness to Agency: An overview of developments in translation studies and some implications for language practice in Africa." *Southern African Linguistics and Applied Language Studies* 29 (3) (2011): 223–241.

———. "An Overview of Recent developments in Translation Studies with Special Reference to the Implications for Bible Translation." *Acta Theologica Supplementum* 2 (2002): 44–69.

Parrat, J. "Time in Traditional African Thought." *Religion* 7 (1977): 118.

Phiri, K. M. "Yao Intrusion into Southern Malawi, Nyanja Resistance, and Colonial Conquest, 1830–1900." *Transafrican Journal of History* 13 (1984): 157–176.

Ryder, A. F. C. "Missionary Activity in the Kingdom of Warri to the Early Nineteenth Century." *Journal of the Historical Society of Nigeria* 2. No. 1 (1960).

Torre, E. "My First Attempts at Translating." *The Jerome Quarterly* 4 (1989): 8.

Unpublished Material

Binnington, J. D. "Where Have All The Bibles Gone?" Internal Note. Edinburgh: The Scottish Bible Society, 1986.

Chilenje, V. *The Origin and Development of the Church of Central Africa Presbyterian (CCAP) in Zambia 1882–2004.* PhD Dissertation. Stellenbosch, South Africa: 2007.

Knight, F. "The History of the National Bible Society of Scotland." Unpublished Research. Edinburgh: The National Bible Society of Scotland, 1937?

Maxwell, I. "An imperishable monument of enlightened judgement the promise of a mighty revolution." Alexander Duff and The General Assembly's Institution in Calcutta, 1830 to 1840." Seminar Paper. New College, University of Edinburgh, 26 June 2001.

Nyirenda, M. "A Critical Review of the Nature and Extent of the Discussion concerning Hebrewisms in African Cultures." MTh. (R) Paper II. CSCNWW, University of Edinburgh, June 2001.

———. "Epistemological Hegemony in the History of Christianity in Africa and the Question of Translatability in the Light of the Thesis of Lamin Sanneh in Translating the Message." MTh. (R) Paper I. CSCNWW, University of Edinburgh, June 2001.

———. "The Exegetical Value of an African Reading of Genesis 4." MCS Thesis, Regent College, 2000.

www.ingramcontent.com/pod-product-compliance
Lightning Source LLC
Chambersburg PA
CBHW070538170426
43200CB00011B/2459